OUTDOOR MAGIC

The Power of Nature Connection

Go ahead — be outdoorable!

Grant Linney

GRANT DOUGLAS LINNEY

FriesenPress

One Printers Way
Altona, MB R0G 0B0
Canada

www.friesenpress.com

Copyright © 2024 by Grant Douglas Linney
First Edition — 2024

All rights reserved.

Illustrator: Paul Schultz
Illustrations on p. 12 and p. 38 by Kainat Ahmad.

Many of these stories describe situations and events that happened decades ago. Since things change over time, the reader must check current procedures (e.g., school board regulations; safety in handling wild animals) before attempting to replicate these events. I encourage you to find the outdoor magic, but you must use common sense.

No part of this publication may be reproduced in any form, or by any means, electronic or mechanical, including photocopying, recording, or any information browsing, storage, or retrieval system, without permission in writing from FriesenPress.

ISBN
978-1-03-831851-0 (Hardcover)
978-1-03-831850-3 (Paperback)
978-1-03-831852-7 (eBook)

1. NATURE, ENVIRONMENTAL CONSERVATION & PROTECTION

Distributed to the trade by The Ingram Book Company

To all the women in my life who have made a real difference, particularly Kate, Nancy, Mary, and Theresa. We need more of a female presence on this beleaguered planet.

To Brian, my longtime friend and canoeing buddy, who passed away earlier this year.

To my outdoor education friends and colleagues over many years: I have learned so much from you and we have made a difference.

To Barkley, my sheepadoodle and fellow nature lover.

ENDORSEMENTS

Part memoir, part manual, Grant Linney's *Outdoor Magic: The Power of Nature Connection* is infused with heart, gentle humour and, ultimately, optimism for humanity, particularly the young, and for the natural world. These timely vignettes from a lifetime of leadership and service in outdoor education affirm that the only sensible way forward for humans is to stay connected to the non-human. Bravo Grant for reminding us how easy and essential that is!
  James Raffan, Speaker, Writer, Explorer

Outdoor Magic is an essential read for all educators, parents, grandparents and nature enthusiasts. Linney provides an inspiring, urgent call to action for us all. We must immerse ourselves and our children in nature so that we can both save it, and ourselves. Through captivating anecdotes of his many outdoor education pursuits, Linney motivates the reader to cultivate the 'ecosystem thinking and feeling' in our youth of today; if we connect with nature directly, we can care about and ultimately save our fragile planet.
  Hilary Coburn, President of the Council of Outdoor Educators of Ontario (COEO)

In a world of ever-increasing environmental problems, we need inspirational stories of how we can forge a real and lasting connection to the very life systems that support us all. Instead of only focusing on reducing harm, we need to relearn how to love this Earth.

In his book *Outdoor Magic*, Grant Linney provides us with authentic, humorous and powerful vignettes of his experiences as an outdoor enthusiast and environmental educator. He shows us how loving, teaching and being in nature can help us create, not just a sustainable future, but a regenerative one.

Jacob Rodenburg, Executive Director, Camp Kawartha

A beautifully written and thought-provoking must-read. Grant Linney's empowering stories are a timely call to action reminding us all that the time to get outdoors and reconnect with the wonders of nature is now. We can do this. We must do this.

Amy Schnurr, Co-Founder & Executive Director, Burlington Green Environmental Association

Outdoor Magic is a collection of engaging stories that remind us of the importance of reconnecting with the natural world. The author's own experiences in nature provide entertaining anecdotes and inspiring examples of outdoor experiential education in action.

Jenna Quinn, Ontario Nature Conservation Science Manager

TABLE OF CONTENTS

Preface: Which Planet Do You Live On?   xi
Introduction   1

PART ONE: PERSONAL ADVENTURES   5
    Introduction to Part One   7
    Early Morning Walk   9
    Across Canada by Train   13
    Canoe Dreams   17
    Biking in Vermont   21
    James Bay Snowshoe Trek   25
    The Mountain River   31
    Hiking in Zion   35
    Moose Music   39
    Sea Kayaking in Haida Gwaii   43
    Travels to Exotic Nature   47

PART TWO: OUTDOOR EDUCATION STORIES   51
    Introduction to Part Two   53
    Night Hike   55
    Mr. Bill   59
    Behaving Like a Bunch of Animals   63
    Trout and Trees   67
    A Bird on Hand   71
    Dawn Watch   75
    Maple Syruping   79
    A Walk in The Dark   83

Magic Spots	87
What's The Matter?	91
Adventure Running	95
Raccoon Circle	99
Loose Parts	103
Serendipity	107
Coast to Coast in 28 Days	111
Students on Ice	115
In the Schoolyard/Local Park	119
Four Credit High School Integrated Outdoor Programs	125

PART THREE: OPINION PIECES ON THE VALUE OF OUTDOOR EDUCATION — 131

Introduction to Part Three	133
Reclaiming The Outdoors For Our Children	135
The Value of Outdoor Education	139

PART FOUR: OTHER VOICES IN SUPPORT OF OUTDOOR EDUCATION — 143

Conclusion	149
About The Fawn on The Front Cover	151
About The Author	153

PREFACE
WHICH PLANET DO YOU LIVE ON?

I am holding two beachball versions of the third rock from the sun. (See photo on back cover.) They are about the same size (twenty centimetres), but they portray our home in dramatically different ways. One is more vivid: an amazing technicolour dream coat representing all 195 (or so) countries on the planet. The other is only a few colours, but it's what our home actually looks like from space—and it's more beautiful.

Now, imagine you are an alien from a universe far, far away. You have never been anywhere near our solar system, but you have this incredible audio technology, and you pick up soundwaves from Earth. No images. Just the spoken word. And so, you learn one of our languages and listen to newscasts every day to learn about humanity. Which of these two planets would you think that we humans live on?

Given that everything including the weather is reported as coming from specific countries, you might well think our world looks like the political globe, with all those defined borders and boundaries created and recreated by humans throughout our brief sojourn on this planet. Very colourful—yes—but also very divisive, fragmented, and arbitrary.

Now, let's consider our real home, the one with just four colours. Two of these colours represent the same substance in three different states of matter: blue is water (liquid) and white is both clouds (gas) and snow (solid). Then, there's the green of living plants and the brown of high and dry. There are no straight lines delineating these colours; they seamlessly flow into one another, and if you rotate the globe in your hands, you are left with the profound impression that it's just one entity. It's all connected.

Aldo Leopold is a famous American philosopher and naturalist from the twentieth century. His words from *A Sand County Almanac* are highly relevant to this introduction:

"We abuse land because we regard it as a commodity belonging to us.

When we see land as a community to which we belong, we may begin to use it with love and respect."

The political globe is all about commodity—what we own, manipulate, control, and destroy at will. This is a world of egocentricity.

The Earth, as viewed from space, is a profound depiction of community. We are all connected. This foundational reality has been lost in our mad pursuit of wealth and material things, but it can be recovered if we see the world for what it really is: a place of ecocentricity. Experiencing outdoor magic—what comes from connecting with nature—is a key step towards this realization.

INTRODUCTION

We are losing the magic. We are losing awe and reverence for our natural surroundings. We are losing a crucial aspect of our lives that provides us with sustenance, meaning and depth, context and even purpose.

We are losing this outdoor magic in two ways. First, the dramatic loss of biodiversity and abundance within the last few decades impoverishes both nature and us. There is a direct link between our obsession with growth and the loss of species. The World Wildlife Fund reports a 69 per cent decline in vertebrate wildlife populations since 1970.[1] Spring mornings are no longer greeted with an abundance of bird and frog song A drive in the country on a summer evening now yields much less bug kill on our car's windshield; while this may initially seem welcome, it is yet another sign of widespread extinction. It is another sign that we are killing our home.

We are also losing this magic because of our addiction to flickering screens in climate-controlled homes, schools, and vehicles. We know far more about our favourite sports teams

---

1 World Wildlife Fund, "69% average decline in wildlife populations since 1970, says new WWF report," last modified October 13, 2022, https://www.worldwildlife.org/press-releases/69-average-decline-in-wildlife-populations-since-1970-says-new-wwf-report

and celebrities than we do about our plant and animal brethren. Our increasingly superficial contact with the outdoors makes us wary of such settings. We are fearful of stings, bites, poisonous plants, and any number of other perceived threats. We bubble wrap our kids. Safety and sanitation override previously natural inclinations to run free, to playfully explore and discover until the streetlights come on. We thus impoverish our very souls.

There is a direct correlation between our estrangement from nature and our failure to believe that we can be active agents in our quest for a healthy and sustainable future. We are distracted. We feel powerless. There is a direct connection between the extinction of outdoor experiences and our own potential extinction as a species.

I believe that we still have time (albeit very limited) to turn things around. This book is about re-establishing our connection with the outdoors and its magic, something with which I am familiar. I have always noticed and enjoyed nature. What started as a childhood interest evolved into a lifetime of multiple outdoor pursuits as well as a wonder-full career of outdoor and environmental education that has now spanned six decades.

Vocation and avocation: all one heartful mission to reconnect with our natural surroundings in ways that spark curiosity, wonder, and activist love. These are my stories—both my fulfilling personal encounters (Part One) and my facilitating others to feel these deep and abiding connections (Part Two). Part Three contains two published opinion pieces I wrote about outdoor education, and Part Four includes the inspiring and insightful words of notable Canadians.

This is my urgent call to action—to re-engage in outdoor magic, to immerse ourselves in nature so that we feel compelled to save it . . . and ourselves.

PART ONE
PERSONAL ADVENTURES

INTRODUCTION
TO PART ONE

While my primary-grade report cards referred to my being a chatterbox in class, I was generally a shy kid. I was into noticing and appreciating nature: the calls of cardinals and blue jays; the robins that returned in March; the grasshoppers and praying mantis in the field en route to and from school in the fall; the willow trees that were first to leaf in the spring and the last to drop their foliage as winter approached.

I have retained this sense of wonder throughout my life. I continue to connect with nature not only physically but mentally, emotionally, and spiritually as well. The following personal stories are my testament to this.

EARLY MORNING WALK

Helen Bambrick was a bird brain, both figuratively and literally. My eccentric neighbour lived with her businessman husband, Ray, a few doors down from me in a modern Chatelaine magazine "House of the Year." Notwithstanding this prestigious fashion accolade, she had an entire downstairs room converted into an aviary for injured birds. She had multiple evergreen and deciduous branches wedged in from floor to ceiling. She changed the floor newspapers daily. She used a medicine dropper to feed her dependents a custom-made, pasty beige, and no-doubt healthy concoction. She constantly caressed and cooed to them. She cared for a variety of local birds, and I learned a great deal about them from her. My favourite was a handsome blue jay named "Comet," who would readily land on my outstretched hand to check me out.

I was fascinated and drawn in. I was thrilled to become her teenaged "chief bird sitter" when she was away. And I shared her intense dislike of cats allowed to roam free through the ravines of our neighbourhood. Their capturing and tormenting of unsuspecting birds were things to which Helen and I both reacted viscerally. On more than one occasion, I would see her wildly brandishing a broom and chasing a cat from her yard. This dramatic scene was accompanied by an indignant shout, "You filthy swine!"

I also had a paper route at the time. It covered an older neighbourhood and a new subdivision that ended abruptly at the Herlbert's great expanse of "undeveloped" private property. I was always intrigued by what lay beyond the dead end that was marked by a fence and a prominent "Private Property: No Trespassing" sign. When I happened to see Mr. Herlbert one day, I asked his permission to come onto his property early one morning to watch birds. He readily agreed. I guess he trusted paperboys who also claimed to be bird lovers.

And so, on Victoria Day in 1966, I had my Westclox Big Ben table clock set to 4:45 a.m.—quite an ungodly hour for a teenage boy. My journal describes "the wonderful fantasia of singing birds" I awoke to. It was nonstop and fully orchestrated. It increased as I came onto the Herlbert's property.

I felt like I was in a foreign wonderland. I walked solo and in silence. But I was not alone, and it was not at all quiet. At first, it was difficult to discern individual bird song from what was a massive chorus. But in my journal, I recorded the distinct whistling of two cardinals, the sharp calls of blue jays, and the rich, throbbing voices of robins. Then it was raucous crows, melodious Baltimore orioles (now known as northern orioles), honking ring-necked pheasants, and what sounded like a mallard duck. Spring peepers and other frogs in a nearby pond added an amphibian soundtrack. A flicker, red-winged blackbird, grackle, brown thrasher, and mourning dove were all sighted. As was a black cat, which I immediately chased and dispatched.

Two cottontail rabbits appeared at different times. I also encountered a raccoon, medium-sized, so I figured it to be a yearling. We both paused and looked at each other. He was wary; I was in awe. When I resumed a slow walk, he climbed up a tree . . . comfortably out of reach. He peered back down at me through his mask. Little did I know then that raccoons would soon become a significant part of my life. Little did I know then that this morning walk was a precursor to dawn walks and paddles that I would later include in my outdoor educator repertoire.

I am amazed at how powerful this moment of connection with other beings remains—even before I recently rediscovered my teen journal. Such memories are a constant nourishment to my soul. *"To be is to be in relation,"* notes Parker Palmer, a modern-day theologian. My early morning hike is a testament to this truth. And, of course, Bird Brain Bambrick heard all about it.

ACROSS CANADA BY TRAIN

I was not taking geography in my Grade 13 year at Lorne Park Secondary School in Mississauga. However, I knew the teachers well enough from previous years to wangle my way onto their June field trip by rail from Toronto to Vancouver and then by ferry to Vancouver Island. This was too exciting to miss.

The first thing that blew me away about this experience was the size of Ontario. The northern evergreen forests just kept going and going and going, kind of like the Energizer Bunny. We left Toronto around 3 p.m. on a Tuesday afternoon, and we did not make it to Winnipeg until Thursday at 10 p.m. We were travelling on a CN transcontinental train; VIA Rail had not yet been created.

Something rare but very Canadian occurred on this Northern Ontario leg of the journey. Heavy rains burst a large beaver dam, with the end result that there was a washed-out rail embankment and a freight train derailment. Yes, our national railway was dependent on our national symbol. We were the first train through after the wreckage had been cleared, and I can remember standing between the railcars, practically being able to reach out and touch pieces of the mangled wreckage.

The next thing that surprised me on this trip was that the great mythological extent of the Canadian prairies was missed. We passed through it overnight. When we awoke on the Friday morning, we were already in the foothills of the Rockies Mountains in Alberta.

For eastern-raised teens, the arrival of the mountains created quite a stir. We moved excitedly from one side of the dining car to the other to catch the latest majestic view, both for our own eyes and for our cameras. We had never seen anything on this grandiose a scale.

As we approached Jasper National Park, I wondered out loud to Miss Wilton, one of our teachers and chaperones, "Do you think I might be able to get permission to board the engine of the train and take pictures from there?"

Miss Wilton knew that photography was my hobby, and she immediately replied, "Go ahead and ask."

I was thrilled by her green light.

When we got to Jasper, I walked up to the diesel at the head of the train. The engineer was just deboarding. When I asked about joining him in the cab, he said, "Well, if it was my decision, I'd say no. But we're switching crews right now, so you might as well wait and ask my replacement."

I did . . . and Bob said yes.

Wow! I may have been nineteen years old, but I felt like an excited kid. To ride in the locomotive of a train is pretty much every boy's dream. For the next couple of hours, Bob and I became fast friends as he explained the engine to me and suggested which side of the train I should be on for the next outstanding view just around the corner.

When we got to Mount Robson, Bob stopped the train to give passengers more time for their photography. He suggested that I climb down off the locomotive and proceed along the tracks

PERSONAL ADVENTURES

so that I could get a picture of the train with Mount Robson in the background. When he saw me squinting because of the bright front light beam, he turned it off. Wow, again!

It was end of day, and the light was fast fading. There I was standing alone on a railway track in the middle of a gorgeous mountain setting, with a transcontinental train idling in front of me. I could have just walked off into the enveloping wilderness. I did not have a tripod, so I slowed down the shutter speed as much as I could (probably 1/30th or may even 1/15th of a second) and I took my pictures. They turned out to be pretty grainy and underexposed, but I was thrilled. I sent a copy of the picture to Bob, and I still have a photo of this moment over my desk.

There are many other great things that happened on this trip, but these are my most lasting memories: the size of Northern Ontario, the burst beaver dam, seeing the mountains for the very first time, and the awesome train ride from the locomotive. And, this trip later evolved into a journey across the country with twenty-four Grade 10 students. . . . You'll find that story in Part Two.

CANOE DREAMS

It's a Saturday morning in late February. My cell phone rings. "Hey, Big G. It's Brian. Where are we going on our canoe trip this August?"

I smile, realizing that I've been waiting for this call. I've already felt an increasing warmth in the sun's rays. I'm tired of this season of snow and ice, of bitterly cold winds, salt-caked slush, and difficult driving. And I'm ready to imagine what I'll be doing when warmth and greenness return.

"Let's do another river," I declare, and Brian laughs agreeably.

All four of us (spouses too) love river trips. Water with a current creates the feeling that we're headed somewhere. Rivers offer more variety than lake paddling, everything from exciting rapids (the first set means no more motorboats or jet skis) to a slow stretch winding its way through a lily-padded marshland. The latter just might host a cow moose and calf scooping up greens, with water noisily rushing back out gigantic, elongated jaws. On a lake, you paddle a broad expanse of open water. On a river, the trees close in on both sides, and the next corner presents a new and inviting view.

Of course, there are preparations to start with. Brian and I consult friends, maps, and canoe trip descriptions as we consider various waterways that fit our seven-to-ten-day time frame. In early summer, our spouses, Nance and Mary, pore over recipes, determining past successes to reprise and new ones to try out. Equipment checks, shopping, and packing follow.

And then, it's time. With two canoes securely lashed on top of Brian's van and several hefty packs loaded into the back, we head somewhere north of Sudbury or Ottawa, to rivers like the Spanish or Missinaibi, the Petawawa or Dumoine. Part of the logistics is paying someone to take our vehicle to the finish. Nance asked Brian about this on one occasion.

"Brian, what do you know about the guy you just entrusted your new van to?"

"His name is Harold" came the reply.

It never ceases to amaze me how immediate the transformation is from rushed urban lives to complete engagement in the here and now of a canoe trip. There are no more lists of household and work chores to do, just being and doing and enjoying the moment. It's like a homecoming.

We are exhilarated by the feel of movement and direction as our paddles cut through the water. We readily adjust to what weather and water conditions present, always curious to see what the next hour and the next bend in the river will reveal. We absorb changing views of our landscape of Canadian Shield, river valley, and boreal forest, immersed in their splendid beauty and calm. We enjoy the flight of a kingfisher or a flock of mergansers as they set off downstream ahead of us. We pause to stretch, relax, and replenish.

PERSONAL ADVENTURES

We scout another set of rapids and decide whether to shoot the whitewater (our first choice), gingerly steer loaded canoes with ropes from the shoreline and shallow waters (a.k.a. lining the rapids), or haul our gear over an adjacent portage. Lining and portaging invariably yield mild grumbles from tired spouses, who note that they must be in some rarified 0.1 per cent of females who'd put up with such hardships. But they complain with a half-smile.

❧

When weather, time of day, or mood dictate, we scout a campsite. Does it have a great view, shelter from the wind, a good fire pit, comfortable space for tents, and a functional outdoor john? Once our selection is made, there's a quick skinny dip from a rocky shoreline. After enduring the initial shock of chilly northern waters, we feel deliciously refreshed and ready to settle in for the remainder of the day.

We pitch our tents on beds of soft pine needles as an indignant red squirrel continuously scolds from overhead. He keeps a close eye on us for the duration of our stay, hopeful that some food might be left out in the open, and ready to repeat his noisy chatter as an unwelcome six o'clock reveille the next morning.

If there is the least suggestion of rain, Brian and I erect a sizeable tarp by means of sturdily lashed paddles and multiple ropes that run in every conceivable direction; we feel great satisfaction as we view our latest version of a taut and weatherproof roof. And then we become immersed in our paperbacks, ensconced in comfortable locations about the campsite where we can occasionally look up and take in yet another fine view of sky and water, rock and forest.

Happy hour presents hors d'oeuvres of smoked oysters on crackers, along with a single malt scotch that is savoured more deeply than it ever could be back home. We then enjoy stove-cooked dinners that include a wine and cheese fondue, Greek pasta, vegetarian shepherd's pie, and the occasional baked chocolate dessert.

We spend cool and bug-free August evenings catching up on each other's lives, reminiscing about various events of this and previous trips together, engaging in a spirited round of Yahtzee, and taking in the silent progression of another sunset. Looming darkness invites us to gaze at another spectacular canopy of stars.

Finally, we retire into our tents, where we read a few more pages by headlamp before yielding to sleep-inducing sounds from outside: the distant roar of a rapids; the haunting calls of loons on a nearby lake; and, sometimes, the steady and strangely reassuring patter of raindrops against our tents as we stretch out, luxuriant in our fatigue from physical exertion, knowing we will remain warm and dry inside our wilderness shelter.

I am adrift in these images of summer magic. An inquiring voice at the other end of the phone line interrupts.

"Big G, are you still there?"

It's a Saturday morning in late February. The days are already growing longer.

BIKING IN VERMONT

I love extended biking trips. I'm not talking about personally hauling all your gear and camping out each night. No, I really enjoy trips where there's a support van to carry your luggage and there's a pre-booked inn waiting to provide you with two wholesome meals (dinner and breakfast), a hot shower, and a comfortable bed. You are unencumbered by extra weight. You are using a means of transport that connects you with the weather and the land.

I love to be with a biking company that looks after all aspects of the trip. You rent bikes in tip-top condition. E-bikes are now an option, often at no extra charge. You have two guides who alternate between driving the support van and being on the road with the group. There's no obligation to remain as one group; you can largely travel at your own pace. You have time to soak it all in.

I have biked in many places, both close to home and farther afield in Canada, the United States, and Europe. My favourite spot is Vermont. The people are friendly and gracious. And the terrain is great, from mainly flat in the south end of the state to more hilly terrain up north, around Stowe.

Bike Vermont (now known as Discovery Bike Tours) offers three- and five-day routes that are safe (e.g., good roads and minimal traffic) and exceptionally scenic. You travel from one idyllic town to another, each with its village square, historic buildings, and general stores that are indeed "general" in terms of the wide variety of merchandise they offer. The spaces between these settlements are decidedly green and inviting. It all adds up to an unbeatable combination of farmed and natural countryside plus these charming small towns. The state is also a major producer of maple syrup and home to more than 100 nineteenth-century wooden covered bridges; there's a good chance that you will come upon at least one of these unique and still-functional bridges during your travels.

The country inns we stay at are another highlight. Friendly innkeepers keep their places in pristine heritage condition, and their hospitality around the dinner and breakfast homecooked meals is outstanding. I'll never forget the then owners of the October Country Inn who capitalized on my sense of humour by offering me a breakfast coffee mug with the following inscribed message: "Hi. My name is Chad and I'll be your coffee mug this morning."

One day can find you really pushing it and going for the extra mileage offered in the itinerary. . . . At times, there's this "right" combination of weather, scenery, and physical well-being that propels you into seizing such an opportunity. Another day will feature an extended lunch at a charming restaurant or pub. Visiting quaint shops is also a frequent option. An early arrival at the inn provides you with the opportunity to relax, read, or socialize.

You have a very large say in the type of experience and the pace you choose. This sort of bike touring is a decidedly civilized way to experience a gorgeous place like Vermont.

JAMES BAY SNOWSHOE TREK

Why would seven males and one female from Southern Ontario opt for a ten-day 210-kilometre snowshoe trek in the middle of winter along the frozen shores of James Bay, from Fort Albany to Moosonee? I think it's safe to say that we were all into outdoor adventure. We'd all been winter camping before, and we loved it. We were also drawn in by the quiet charisma, outstanding knowledge, and impressive experience of our leader, C. K. Macdonald.

Craig has a longstanding fascination with the traditions of Indigenous peoples living in Northern Ontario. He interviewed several hundred First Nations Elders about their traditional ways of living in the woods. He became particularly interested in their pre-snowmobile travel skills. This trip was intended to replicate a winter technique involving snowshoes and long tumplines that are attached in a loop to pull sleds and toboggans loaded with food and gear. The tumpline is usually run across the top of one's chest and shoulders. Arms are wrapped around the tails of the tumpline to reduce shoulder strain. In this region, there were often no dog teams—just human power.

As non-agricultural hunter-gathers, the Cree needed to disperse during winter when food was scarce. They would travel in groups of up to twenty to their ancestral hunting territories. The group would consist of a few prime hunters plus their families. They would focus on half of their territory for three to five years, then switch over to the other half. There would be regular forays out of a base camp to hunt and to check traplines. Their diet was primarily fish and meat. Furs were processed by scraping the pelts and then stretching them on either wooden forms or hoops depending on the type of animal. During spring, the furs were carried out to larger and more central settlements where they would be traded for goods and supplies. Talk about knowing how to live with nature in a difficult environment.

Our travel averaged twenty kilometres a day. We had obtained a recent satellite image of the area to mark our progress. While the windswept and wide-open conditions of the shoreline meant we were seldom in deep snow, hauling our heavy food and gear in minus-twenty degrees Celsius conditions was no easy task. We had to constantly adjust the number of layers we wore according to both work output and weather. We were also fortunate to have a warm March sun for most of our days. There were several occasions when we were wearing both toques and sunscreen. We also quickly learned that our strenuous daily efforts could lead to dehydration; we needed to compensate for this by drinking liquids continuously.

※

Our travel efforts were matched by the amount of time and energy we expended to set up and break camp daily. As per Cree traditions going back to the nineteenth century, we camped well inshore, where we had access to firewood and poles of sufficient length. Each day, we cut eighteen-foot-long poles to set up two large canvas wall tents. We used shovels to dig the front third of the tent down to bare ground, piling up this snow at the back of the tent to construct an elevated platform for our insulated pads and sleeping bags. This allowed us to sleep in warmer air because the hot air from our stove rose to the ridge of the tent.

We installed our sheet-metal wood stove on bare ground at the front of the tent. A long stove pipe stack directed any sparks away from our highly flammable tent walls. We also needed to cut a third of a cord of dead firewood for cooking and overnight heat. Spruce, tamarack, and poplar were our main fuels, with the last type providing the most heat when found dry. There were no puddles inside the tent: a proper setup meant that there was an equilibrium established, where cold met heat without melting more snow.

We were quite tired by the end of each day. But we were also warm. Temperatures outside the tent would go down to minus forty degrees Celsius, but the inside temperature just below the ridge pole would register a balmy plus twenty degrees Celsius. This made for a luxurious morning ritual: putting on warm and dry day clothing that had hung overnight from a ridgepole clothesline.

The nightly challenge was who would rise from their warm sleeping bag to stoke a dying fire. There was a friendly competition among us as to who would sleep in Craig's tent because we knew that if the temperature dropped only a few degrees in the night, Craig would be on it immediately. The rest of us would more than gladly defer to his heat-driven initiative.

Yes, our daily routine was strenuous, but we very much enjoyed the challenge, the comradery, the vast and beautifully bleak landscape, and the cultural traditions we were reprising. As to the last point, we occasionally met a Cree fellow zooming by on a snowmobile. He would stop and chat and no doubt report our progress to family and friends. He seemed quite bemused by us. "Why are you doing this?" was a very common question.

Our last night out was the most memorable. There was a full moon that illuminated the smoke coming out of the tent stove pipes. It also cast soft tree shadows onto the snow. It was bright enough that one could read a book. And then, there was a magnificent full-fledged dome of aurora borealis, continuously moving and shimmering across the sky. What a fitting finale to a memorable expedition.

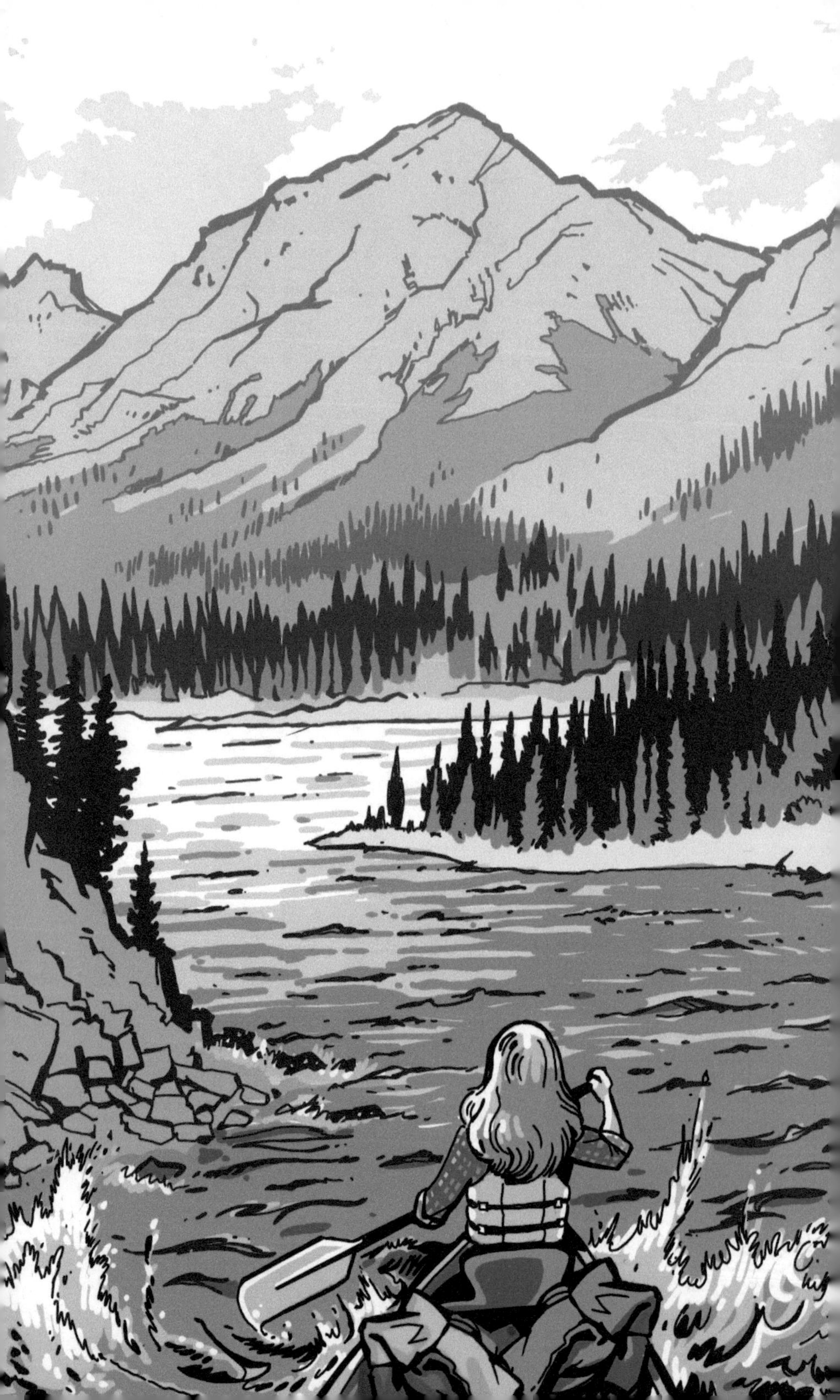

THE MOUNTAIN RIVER

Our de Havilland Twin Otter float plane was jam-packed: one seventeen-foot canoe strapped to each pontoon plus one more wedged inside the cabin, along with half our tripping gear and half our party of ten. Yes, it took two flights.

We flew in from Norman Wells, located on the shores of the Mackenzie River in the Northwest Territories. We had a very smooth landing on Willow Handle Lake, a small body of water high up in the mountains. No wind. Very calm. And when the plane left us, there was a deep and peaceful silence. We were on our own.

At an end of the lake was a grassy and shallow waterway, which we quickly named "Push Me, Pull Me Creek" because we spent a lot of time doing these very things. Then it got larger—still officially a creek by NWT standards, but now a small river, complete with whitewater to navigate. Since we were in a narrow and deep V-shaped valley, our vision forward and to the sides was limited.

※

A few days later, we rounded a corner and everything dramatically opened up. We were presented with a stunning panorama of the Mountain River, and it was immediately clear that this was a most fitting name. I remember feeling breathless with awe. I remember tears running down my cheeks. I remember feeling so small amid this magnificent backdrop. While the grand scale remained for the duration of the trip, I shall never forget this initial revelatory moment.

We settled into a daily routine of nutritional and plentiful meals (including freshly caught fish), breaking camp, travel, and then setting up in a new location down river. August temperatures were on the cool side (no bugs!), so we were dressed in layers with long sleeves. On one occasion, hail collected on the splash cover of our canoes. Yes, this was big water—lots of standing waves—so full splash covers over the tops of the canoes were necessary, as were various canoe strokes, including braces, pries, and draws. This being my first far northern river, I learned a lot about back ferrying, paddling backward in unison with your canoe partner so that you slow down the speed at which you approach rapids. And if you angle the canoe slightly as you back paddle, you can move sideways across the river, better lining oneself up for a good approach to upcoming rapids. What a cool manoeuvre!

Our adventure also included backcountry hikes across Barrenlands scree. That was why we brought along sturdy hiking shoes. We gained even more spectacular views on these land expeditions, and it was a nice break from the demands of big river navigation.

My photos include a distant view of caribou, an Arctic loon, and a normal-sized Swiss Army knife that is dwarfed by the gigantic grizzly paw print around it. There are also images of the five magnificent canyons that closed in the river as we paddled through them. Oh, and there's also this very expansive rainbow that occupies the entire skyline in a spot where the river widens.

My dominant memory of this trip is one of scale. Everything was huge except for us. I was humbled and, on numerous occasions, tried to imagine being in the same exact spot in the middle of the winter. I was convinced that this setting would remain just as grand at any time of year. It was such a privilege to visit it for this fleeting moment.

HIKING IN ZION

I have visited several impressive national parks in the United States, but I have one clear favourite: Zion National Park in southwestern Utah. The easiest way to reach this park from a distance is to fly into Las Vegas and rent a car from there. Talk about dramatic contrasts. "The strip" in Las Vegas is, for many, the epitome of Western decadence with its neon lights, hotel casinos, glamorous shows, and flashy water displays in the middle of the Nevada desert. Zion is the opposite. It is the ultimate in gorgeous natural beauty, serenity, and reverence. It has two particularly "awe-some" features that stand out for me.

First, there are these massive red canyon walls that assume a rich aethereal glow when light reflects off a nearby rock face.

Second, the main road through the park is at the bottom of the canyon; magnificent rock walls surround you. You are very much in the midst of this wonder, and there are several parking lots from which you can take a variety of exceptionally scenic hikes ranging in both length and degree of difficulty.

The trails with limited change in elevation tend to be short and to follow or cross the beautiful Virgin River. The one exception to this is the Canyon Overlook Trail on the east side of the park, just past the Zion-Mount Carmel Tunnel; this underground passage is a 1.8-kilometre-long roadway blasted through an imposing mountain face. It's well worth going here, not only so that you can experience the impressively engineered one-lane tunnel when the traffic is heading your way, but also so you can see how the rock changes dramatically from rich-red canyon walls to more rounded mountains that are a greyish white. The Canyon Overlook Trail is only a 1.6-kilometre round trip, but it presents this landscape change quite well.

There is one longer "flat" route that requires hip waders and hiking poles; these are available from a local expedition outfitter. This full day's journey begins with an easy trek along a very open route known as the Riverside Walk. Once you reach the end of this walk, you don your hip waders and use the sturdy hiking poles to navigate the boulder-strewn Virgin River. You head upstream through "The Narrows," where the canyon walls close in around you and you feel like you are entering a great cathedral. This hike comes with a warning: flash thunderstorms well upstream can occasionally lead to huge floods and unfortunate drownings in this narrow canyon, but I'm not trying to scare you away. If you're up for a full day of strenuous exercise, this trek is a wonderful experience. Just be sure to carefully check the weather forecast before heading out.

There are a few hike options featuring gentle climbs that take up to half a day. The Watchman is one such ascent along the cliff sides of a minor canyon and through evergreen forests. It leads you to a breathtaking panoramic view of several sizeable mountains. This was my first wife's favourite hike. She enjoyed the pace. She loved the view, particularly of the singular Watchman peak. When Nancy was undergoing chemotherapy, the Watchman was a centrepiece of her daily meditation practice. We made one last trip to Zion two months before Nancy passed away, and she was downright triumphant when she was able to complete this fine hike one last time.

PERSONAL ADVENTURES

During earlier visits, Nancy and I were able to take on more strenuous ascending hikes, such as Observation Point and Angel's Landing. They were challenging, but we were rewarded with spectacular views that made us feel both humble and reverent. A favourite feature of Angel's Landing is "Walter's Wiggles" (named after a former park superintendent), a massive and very impressive set of hand-hewn stone steps that run back and forth in short segments over quite a significant change in elevation.

For our hikes, we carried several litres of water and nutritious snacks (e.g., trail mix, cheese and crackers). At the end of the day, we would return to our accommodations in Springdale, a small town just outside the south entrance. This settlement also features a good variety of restaurants where we could relax after a wonderful day of hiking.

The best time of year to visit Zion is October/November and March/April. With temperatures in the mid-teens, it is ideal hiking weather and it's uncrowded.

You can really let this magical place sink in.

MOOSE MUSIC

It's 5:30 on a Saturday morning in late September. I am driving across Algonquin Park to an early rendezvous with six other adventurers. A full moon follows above and behind me, occasionally vanishing behind a sharp bend in Highway 60, then reappearing to cast long, velvet shadows and to illuminate plumes of mist rising from glassy expanses of water. There is a surreal lighting to this seemingly abandoned stretch of road. But I am not alone. The eyes of a fisher catch my headlights before he disappears into the bush. A fox hurries across the road and into the darkness. Even though I am still in my car, I already feel a spell of enveloping wilderness.

As moonlight yields to growing dawn, five nature photography students and Dave, our instructor, gather at the east gate parking lot. This is prime moose rutting season. Our purpose is to call these creatures, to lure them into the open, so that we can capture their image.

We begin travelling up and down the access road from Highway 60 to Lake Opeongo. We stop at various points, and Dave raises a cone-shaped piece of black poster board to his lips. The calls to lovemaking begin with two short descending grunts. Then there is a long, mournful ascending and descending call, gracefully accentuated by a corresponding arc in Dave's standing posture as he attempts primal connection with his mammalian brethren. Two more cow-like descending grunts. Then silence. We anxiously await some reply from the forest depths. The silence continues.

Then, a response from the road. Other cars stop. Their occupants see our small group, our tripods, and our cameras with long lenses. They see our Tilley-hat-clad leader doing his seemingly ancient, ritualistic performance, and they hear his haunting calls. Like us, they are here to see moose, and so they emerge from their vehicles, hopeful that we have some inside knowledge as to the whereabouts of our common quarry . . . and that Dave does indeed know what he is doing. Our group becomes a crowd.

There is still no response from the forest depths.

We move on and, at our next stop, we hike a short distance up a dew-laden path marked by recent moose tracks and droppings. Once again, Dave makes amorous overtures to unseen occupants of the surrounding bush. Once again, we listen. This time, out of sight of the access road and other hopeful human eyes, we are greeted with a deep and utter quiet. Strangely enough, I do not feel disappointed.

⁂

I am late to my group's afternoon meeting spot, and they have left without me. There are many trail options, so I explore the woods close to the parking lot and enjoy warm, summer-like weather and vibrant fall colours at their height. As time passes, I decide to try out my own moose calls. With a little practice, I feel that I can do a respectable rendition of the two descending grunts. I even manage to attract a group of curious chickadees that flit about in nearby branches, investigating my noisy presence from various distances and angles.

I hear my group chatting as they return to the parking lot. I decide to try out my newly acquired skills. It takes a few calls to get their attention. Much to my surprise, Dave affectionately responds. What do I do now? I know that the longer call is far beyond my fledgling abilities, that any attempt at such a higher plane of foreplay would immediately expose me as a fraud, so I limit myself to the perfunctory side of love. I emit two more grunts with as much expression as I can muster. Dave takes out the rack of antlers he carries with him and bangs it up against a clump of saplings, simulating the response that an eager male might make to the calls of a potential mate.

What do I do now? Johnny One Note sticks to his tried-and-true grunts. Then I remember that they are not going to come into the woods to find an aroused creature that happens to weigh in at 1,600 pounds. No, they are waiting for me to come to them so that they can photograph me in my full splendour. I deliberately break a few branches as I make my way awkwardly towards them. Dave finally spots me, and I am grateful that my attempted ruse is over. Ensuing inquiries as to whether or not I can swim suggest that the group has had enough of my antics.

※

Next morning, we are again driving the Lake Opeongo Road in our quest for still elusive lovers. Once again, our efforts bear no fruit. Dave leads our group of vehicles towards Mizzy Lake in the west end of the park, but as we drive along Highway 60, I grow increasingly restless. I recall his comment about having days as a nature photographer when you have no luck and then experiencing other times when everything seems in sync. I then realize that, for me at this particular time, synchronicity means taking advantage of different opportunities that are presenting themselves. And so, I break away from our small convoy. I turn around and head back a kilometre to a view that caught my attention just moments before: a tall white pine is strikingly silhouetted against a sun-drenched morning mist. At first, I just stand there and take in what my senses bring to me, for I realize that I cannot capture on film the subtlety of this lighting and my awe of the moment. A few minutes later, I turn my attention to other features around me. I take photographs of verdant cedar fronds and deeply reddened maple leaves whose edges are still clad in morning frost. I relax. I enjoy another outstanding fall day. I feel a marvellous and full sense of peace and belonging.

Later that morning, I get my moose shot. I unexpectedly catch him in broad daylight as he is about to cross the highway. I have his full profile, antlers and all. He is in black silhouette against a striking yellow diamond background. And underneath his proud image are the words "For 30 km."

SEA KAYAKING IN HAIDA GWAII

Situated off the northwest coast of British Columbia in the Hecate Strait, Haida Gwaii (previously known as the Queen Charlotte Islands) consist of approximately 150 islands of varying sizes. The largest are Moresby and Graham Islands. It is considered a temperate rainforest; it gets an annual average rainfall of more than 800 millimetres, but not during our August 1986 trip. We had ten days of glorious sun and calm seas . . . maybe thirty minutes of rain in total. So much for the fabled "Misty Isles."

The best way to experience this archipelago is by means of kayak. The two-person Klepper sea kayak is a German creation from the early twentieth century. Apparently, it was used during World War II for clandestine military operations at night. A "skin" is stretched around its sturdy wooden frame with a thick rubber bottom and a heavy-duty canvas upper deck. It is completely collapsible. It comes with a foot-operated rudder for steering as well as for stability in windy conditions.

There is much to learn about our sea kayaks. There is a real art to using the limited space at the bow, stern, and midships (between the two paddlers) to store all our food and gear . . .

and still have room to slide ourselves in. Once you get a feel for both the boat and the two-bladed long paddles, your movement through the water is both stable and efficient. Then you learn how to sail this craft. Yes, it has a main and gib sail, and lessons are given about their operation. It's quite the exhilarating feeling to be sailing a kayak, particularly in such a gorgeous setting.

Haida Gwaii is rich and verdant. Giant western cedars dominate the landscape and provide the gorgeous raw material for Haida lodges, totems, canoes, and paddles. The surrounding waters are full of sea life, the main staple of a Haida diet. The people thrived in this pristine and bounteous environment until their population was decimated by European diseases. Once vibrant settlements have all but disappeared, with the notable exception of a few magnificent but heavily weathered and fallen totems.

Paddling through Haida Gwaii is like visiting an isolated heaven on Earth. There is the monumental majesty of those western cedars, with bald eagles looking down at the waters from lofty vantage points. Red-eyed oyster catchers populate the rock shoreline below; their beaks are specially designed to crack open oyster shells to access the soft treat inside. The forest floor is soft and moss-covered, with fallen trees in various stages of returning their nutrients to the soil. On our trip, we saw deer and black bear on the larger islands. The sunsets were consistently gorgeous. One evening, we witnessed a full moonrise over the ocean. This is a place of silent majesty.

We were initially a group of ten strangers, but we quickly became good friends, enjoying each other's company. Bob Sutherland was our wonderful and very capable lead guide. Each morning began with his informative map talk concerning our plans for the day. His background in marine biology enabled him to share all manner of fascinating knowledge with us. When we reached our evening campsite, he snorkeled in the nearby waters and brought up an ocean bounty of abalone, sea urchins, and other creatures. He also took us on guided walks of the unique world of intertidal zones, where creatures are adapted to a twice-daily cycle of water (high tide) and no water (low tide). His knowledge of tide tables also meant that we never made the mistake of leaving a kayak within the zone of high tides. He also took us on gorgeous forest walks past icy freshwater creeks and up to mountain lakes. On Hot Springs Island, Bob led us to its namesake, where we soaked in warm waters amidst a magnificent backdrop of rocks, trees, and coastal mountains.

We ate very well on this trip. Breakfast and lunch were designed to be fast and nutritious. Breakfast featured a hardy six-grain cereal along with brown sugar, powdered milk, and powdered orange juice. Lunch consisted of rye bread, pepperoni sticks, cheese, and peanut butter. Supper was a sumptuous affair, often featuring freshly caught abalone (deshelled and fried in a pan) and coho salmon (cooked in a wonderful variety of mouth-watering ways).

We were saddened to see occasional vast clearcutting scars in the otherwise uninterrupted forest. Now, almost forty years later, most of Haida Gwaii is protected land. And rightfully so.

TRAVELS TO EXOTIC NATURE

Antarctica, the Galapagos Islands, and Costa Rica

As an Al Gore-trained Climate Reality Project leader, I have now delivered more than 1,000 volunteer presentations on climate change to a wide variety of audiences. This is the greatest existential problem ever faced by humankind, and we have a very short window of opportunity for decisive and comprehensive action. By far the most impactful actions will be from government-led system change. Examples of this include legislation that renders old technologies obsolete (e.g., incandescent light bulbs, the burning of fossil fuels) and that incentivizes our adoption of new low-carbon technologies (e.g., government grants to assist with greening one's home and/or purchasing an electric vehicle). There's a lot that individuals can do to make a difference, but we need our governments to take a much more active leadership role. They must provide inspirational leadership, legislate much-needed changes, and help citizens with the costs of these changes.

Westerners love to visit other parts of the world via air travel. The good news is that, within the next decade, air travel will be emissions free. In the meantime, flying has an egregiously high carbon footprint. We thus need to practise being "infrequent" flyers.

I am afraid that my personal record of air travel is not at all exemplary. In 2017, my wife and I visited Antarctica. In 2019, we visited Ecuador and the Galapagos. In 2023, my new wife and I visited Costa Rica. I have also been to the Arctic twice (2018 and 2019) with a Canadian organization called Students on Ice. That's one heck of a big carbon footprint.

※

Antarctica comprises the most outstanding landscape for me—huge masses of ice and snow standing in magnificent silence. And then there's the opportunity to meet its occupants, up close and personal.

Three kinds of penguins—Gentoo, Adélie, and Chinstrap—all dressed up in their evening formal wear. While there, one Gentoo came right up to me as I sat on the beach; his curiosity got the better of him and he landed up pecking on my boot.

The bellicose elephant seals were found lolling on the beach. I wonder whether these massive creatures are what gave movie director George Lucas the inspiration for Jabba the Hut in Star Wars.

A formidable threesome of humpback whales approached our boat. They were barely at the surface, but we still made out their huge shapes. The occasional spout from their blow holes was also most impressive.

We also came upon leopard seals: their faces look lovely, but they are incredibly quick and deadly carnivores. Beware, all penguins!

PERSONAL ADVENTURES

※

From the isolated islands of the Galapagos evolved a marvellous and unique array of creatures—giant tortoises and other prehistoric reptiles, crabs, the blue-footed booby, sea turtles, and colourful fish. Snorkelling enabled us to get up close and personal. No wonder Charles Darwin loved this archipelago.

※

Costa Rica—my recent and first winter getaway to a warm location may not be my last. The gorgeous Pacific sunsets. A river boat tour that yielded prehistoric-looking crocodiles, white-faced monkeys and howler monkeys, iguana, bats, and a variety of bird life. A rainforest tour that brought us face to face with sloths, tree frogs, and toucans. . . . The sloths appeared to be practising the slow, articulated movements of tai chi. They are so deliberate and graceful. The amazing thing about the tree frogs is that they camouflage perfectly with the vegetation. It takes an experienced guide to notice what we would have otherwise walked by. And then, with a guide's gentle handling, they can suddenly transform into an iridescent green with bright orange feet and eyes . . . an amphibious jewel.

My personal love of nature has only broadened and deepened as a result of these adventures, and, realizing how fortunate I am to have had them, I feel compelled to share my photographs and stories about these travels with as many others as possible. Each of these places has offered me wonderful experiences in unique, distinct, and outstanding environments. They have been "other-worldly."

We are part of a much-varied heaven on Earth. We are part of a magnificent natural and fragile environment, which we must care for. It is not a commodity belonging to us but a community of which we are all a part. And we are destroying it.

PART TWO

OUTDOOR EDUCATION STORIES

INTRODUCTION
TO PART TWO

I was born to be an outdoor educator. I love sharing the outdoors with others, particularly children. I love facilitating their encounters with nature. This started as a teen Scout leader and day camp counsellor. When I was twenty-one, I had several summer job offers. My parents were disappointed I chose to work at a boys' camp in Haliburton, Ontario. Camp Kandalore was directed by a very charismatic and gifted University of Toronto physical education professor by the name of Kirk Wipper. It turned out to be the most wonderful time of my life. Four summers there opened me up to this marvellous world of outdoor experiential education (OEE): the amazingly different ways that it can be expressed, its transformative impact on learners, and the very skilled and dedicated staff who were its practitioners—all within an outdoor milieu that I totally loved. This was the beginning of what became six decades of wonderful engagement "in the field," working for conservation authorities, school boards, the Ontario government, an independent school, and as a volunteer.

The 1970s and '80s were the heyday of OEE in Ontario. We grew, we thrived, and we celebrated. I remember when the initial stirrings of restraint came to our profession. Two colleagues with the Hamilton Wentworth and the Peterborough district school boards were the first to experience cutbacks, and they warned the rest of us. But we did not really understand until it came to be our turn. And so, we were stunned by the fiscal "realities" of the early 1990s. Our hearts knew that OEE was uniquely powerful on multiple fronts, but, try as we might, we were unable to effectively articulate this to school board trustees and administrators charged with balancing a budget. We became regarded as a frill. There were many closures, including the field centre where I worked at the time.

And so, for seven long years, I was "out" of OEE. Two were spent pursuing a master's of education in curriculum studies at the University of Toronto. Virtually every course I took became a ringing endorsement of OEE. I knew I was on the right track, but I had to survive five years in the "wilderness" of high school classroom teaching before I could return home, this time with one of Canada's leading independent schools—Upper Canada College and its Norval Outdoor School—where I once again thrived in the midst of outdoor learning. The stories that follow both pre- and post-date my indoor classroom hiatus.

NIGHT HIKE

In my first year of teaching, I worked as an instructor at the Albion Hills Conservation Field Centre, an outdoor education centre northwest of Toronto. Students would come for a week, live at the centre, and learn about the environment in this 1,100-acre setting and through all four seasons. I lived and breathed this place. I was enthralled by how engaged kids became with this "learning by doing" experiential approach outside the four walls of the traditional classroom.

In late March of that first year, I was working with a group of Grade 7 and 8 students from St. Daniel Separate School in Toronto. It was a Thursday evening. This was the group's fourth and final night at Albion, and many were no doubt running on fumes by this time. When I took them out on a night hike around nine o'clock, I had forty energetic and excitable students noisily following me. I tried to get them to quiet down, to relinquish their animated engagement with one other in favour of opening their senses to Albion's still snow-covered winter milieu. I had no success.

And so, I took off on them. I ran away and then circled back so I was close by but unseen. There was immediate silence. Then a few of the girls started to cry and I felt compelled to re-emerge. I explained why I had resorted to this action, and this time when I asked them to be quiet and listen, they did. Some were impressed with how quiet and still it was. Others seemed impatient and ready to finish the hike, so we did.

I was surprised when three boys came up to me at bedtime to recount how much they had enjoyed the hike and said, "Wouldn't it be nice if we could go out there again?" Even though I was a rookie, I was already inoculated with the standard teacher "Yes, but . . ." reply, so they joined their classmates to settle in for a night's sleep. When I later told the classroom teacher about the wishes of the three students, he looked me in the eye and immediately responded, "Go ahead and do it if you'd like to."

I was startled, then excited.

And so, shortly after midnight, I awoke three city boys named Joe, Chris, and Frank, and took them back out into the night environs of Albion Hills. We were out there for a good hour and a half, having no particular plan for what or how or when. We opened our senses. We whispered only occasionally. We heard two owls calling through the deep and peaceful silence. We felt the mild dampness of a late winter night on our faces. We made out the shapes of the trees and bushes, trails, and frozen streams amazingly well, thanks to the snow reflection and our quickly adapting black-and-white night vision. We walked and periodically just stood still or sat down to soak it all in. We felt an unspoken kinship with each other and with our surroundings. We seemed to be caught up in a reverential awe of something so much larger than ourselves.

The experience was not over when we returned to the field centre. We all seemed to be deeply moved by this time, though later attempts to verbalize its impact always fell short. Joe wrote me letters for the next four years. While the night hike was seldom mentioned, it was clear that this shared event was the base of our bond.

Many years later and after moving on to other outdoor education centres, I was conducting an environmental awareness workshop for teachers back at Albion Hills. One of my activities involved asking participants to think back to some positive experience in the natural environment. We then shared these memories and speculated as to why they were still so powerful and what meaning they had for us now. One young teacher spoke of the impact on his teaching of a late-night hike at Albion some fifteen years earlier. It turned out to be Chris. We both revelled in the retelling of our story that evening.

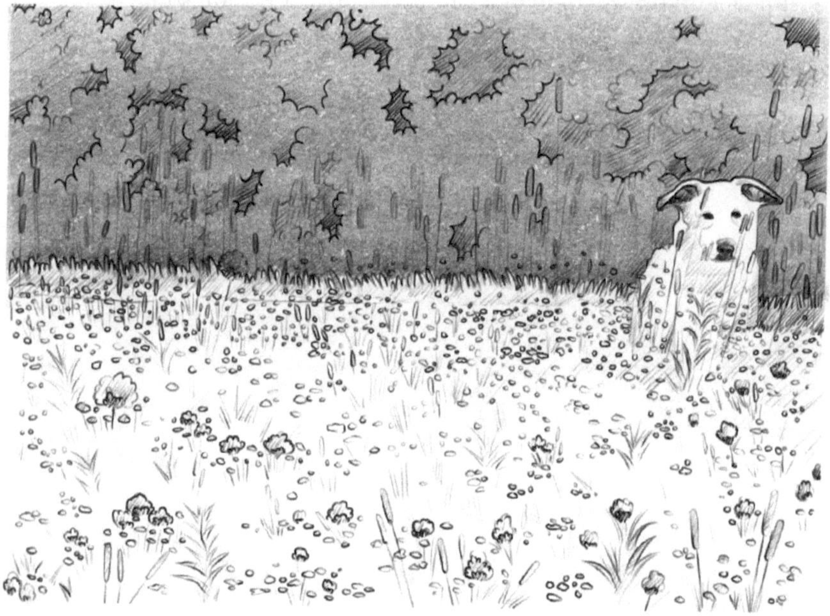

MR. BILL

I went into the local pet store to buy a guppy for my "pond in a jar" demonstration ecosystem. I must have come down with a case of dyslexia that day because I came out with a puppy instead. He was one of four in an unwanted litter. The mother was a breeding golden retriever, and the father was a stranger in the night. The results of this unexpected rendezvous were totally adorable, and I almost bought his sister too. But I phoned a vet friend, and he advised me to purchase just one.

"Otherwise," Dr. Bob said, "they will become dog dogs, not people dogs."

So, I purchased one puppy for the grand total of twenty-five dollars. . . . I still have the receipt.

The next step was coming up with a name, and I immediately recalled teens at the summer camp where I worked constantly exclaiming, "Oh, no, Mr. Bill!" They were referring to a then-famous character on Saturday Night Live. I had never seen this segment, but the name stuck.

I needed to get permission from my boss to bring Mr. Bill to work, to the outdoor education day centre where I was at the time. He readily agreed, something that would now be highly unlikely for any number of reasons (e.g., allergies).

The final step was to integrate him into our programs—for example, an animal ecology hike through forest and meadow.

"Mr. Bill, what do you call the skin of a tree?"

This was followed by an eager and immediate response. "Bark!" he'd reply.

"Good, Mr. Bill! Now put your paws up on this maple tree." My dog would readily obey.

"What does this bark feel like?"

"Rough!" he'd say, with some translation assistance from me.

As I'd lead a class of keen and excited primary students through our outdoor classroom, the probing question/immediate-answer routine would continue.

"Mr. Bill, who chases rabbits?"

"Wolf!" came the reply.

"Mr. Bill, what do you call the top of this building?"

"Roof!" I'd repeat.

Mr. Bill would get so excited about this routine that I could tell he was about to sneeze. At this point, I'd ask him what the name of one of the Seven Dwarfs was. He'd enthusiastically and somewhat involuntarily emit his reply.

"Sneezy!" I'd say. "You have such a great memory, Mr. Bill!"

Then came the real test. We'd stop at a beech tree, which has a smooth grey bark, sort of like the skin of an elephant. I'd ask Mr. Bill to put his paws up on the tree before asking him what it feels like. The teachers were peering curiously at us, wondering what was coming next.

"Rough!" my dog would say.

"No, no, Mr. Bill," I'd exclaim. "You're barking up the wrong tree!"

The teachers would then groan and shake their heads while the kids remained impressed.

"Gee, Mr. Linney, how did you teach Mr. Bill all these words?"

Mr. Bill looked like a fit and slender yellow lab. He loved kids and exploring the outdoors. He would always lead our animal ecology hike, nose constantly sniffing the ground.

"If he could talk even more, Mr. Bill would use his nose to say that a fox crossed the trail an hour ago or that three deer were here early this morning. He travels with his nose. He learns what's been going on through his nose."

When we would stop along the trail, Mr. Bill would immediately sit beside me. I'd show him a stick I had just picked up. Then I'd show it to the kids and ask them to note its distinctive features before I threw it away as far as I could. Meanwhile, Mr. Bill remained seated by my side. He would not move until I'd say, "Go!"

Off he'd charge and, yes, after some looking about, Mr. Bill would indeed return with the same stick. I'd then ask my class how he could find this stick out of all the ones lying around.

"He can smell you on the stick," one declared triumphantly, and the others nodded in agreement.

I would note how wild animals depend on their sense of smell even more than Mr. Bill—a key to detecting both food and danger, and, quite simply, a survival strategy.

❧

When I subsequently visited the schools that had come to our outdoor centre, the kids would often come up to me and say, "Hey, I know you. . . . You're Mr. Bill's owner!" or "You're the one with the talking dog!"

How fondly I remember my constant companion and teaching colleague of many years ago!

Thanks, Mr. Bill. You were so good at teaching kids about connections.

BEHAVING LIKE A BUNCH OF ANIMALS

Many outdoor education centres have activities known as "simulations"—where students are asked to get into role play as much as safety and common sense allow. One of the student favourites is "Animal Instincts for Survival," where Grade 7 and up students are asked to behave, well, like a bunch of animals. When laughter and animated conversations immediately follow this introduction, I draw a sharp distinction between "party animals," who make all kinds of noise and do lots of hijinks . . . and wild animals, who do not at all wish to be seen or heard.

All animals must find four things in order to survive: food, water, shelter, and space. For water, all animals in this simulation must find x number of water stations (i.e., blue T-bars firmly planted in the ground with a heavy-duty plastic punch on each one, which, using your food and water card, leaves a distinctive mark). The larger the animal, the more water you require—the more of these stations you must find.

For food, your success depends on finding your symbolic diet. For herbivores (wearing green pinnies) and omnivores (blue pinnies), one looks for plant stations (i.e., green T-bars, each with a distinctive punch). Omnivores may also hunt smaller mammals (mice in yellow pinnies), and carnivores (red pinnies) hunt any herbivore or omnivore. Depending on animal size, there is a quota of food that one must meet to survive.

For shelter, all animals have enemies who can hunt them down. Even the carnivores must keep a wary eye for the hunter and for disease. They also want to hide from potential prey until the last possible moment. If you are tagged by an enemy, you must give up one of your life tags (i.e., poker chips on a shower curtain ring) as food for that predator. The more enemies you have in the simulation, the more life tags you are given to start with, and you must keep at least one to survive. Carnivores, for example, start the simulation with three tags; mice start with six.

For space, a large area with well-defined boundaries and a mixture of meadow and forest is ideal.

※

For the simulation to really work, I created a series of "S words for survival" that students are to follow:

Safety: This is not a track meet; watch where you are going and no tree climbing.

Silence: You want to notice others before they notice you.

Solo: Groups attract attention; no animal in this simulation travels in groups (a herd of mice?).

Senses: Use sight and sound to detect others before they notice you.

Stealth/Sneaky: Don't find your food and water by excessive movement; running is a last resort.

※

Outdoor educators use a "butterfly" metaphor to run effective experiential programs. One wing is the prep—making sure that everyone fully understands the task at hand. This includes answering any student questions, usually with, "What would a wild animal do in the situation you have just described?" The body of the butterfly is the actual event, full on. The other wing is the debrief afterward.

When the actual simulation is being run, I feel great satisfaction from the students' successful application of the S words. This is what makes it so much more than a glorified game of tag.

The debrief is what really consolidates student learning. After everyone reports in the number of life tags they have left and the number of food and water they found, I ask the following sample questions:

Did you survive?

What surprised you?

What was your biggest challenge?

What would have happened if we had started with equal numbers of herbivores, omnivores, and carnivores? Here, we would discuss the concept of a "pyramid of numbers."

Depending on grade level and curriculum links, the classroom teacher can also do all kinds of follow-up activities back at the school. Creative writing, discussions, and assignments concerning food webs and human impacts on wildlife all provide fertile ground.

Thanks to Frank Glew, an outstanding outdoor educator from Waterloo, Ontario, who first created this wonderful simulation. Well done, Frank!

Stonefly Nymph

TROUT AND TREES

It's the evening before we do our stream study, and I am introducing it to a visiting group of Grade 5s in the classroom of our outdoor education centre. I write the following on the board:
TRUE OR FALSE?
TROUT NEED TREES

You need to understand that this question is rather jarring and something of a brain stretcher for ten- and eleven-year-olds. There are many puzzled and perplexed looks. I take a vote and the class is evenly split between true, false, and the very Canadian "undecided."

Then I ask them to explain their votes. Some students are quite literal: "I've never seen a trout in a tree."

And then there are those who suspect that their teacher (me) is up to something: "Now, wait a minute," the interior monologue goes. "I don't know how, but I think there's some truth about trout needing trees. Besides, I think Mr. Linney is trying to trick us!"

It seems that I have something of a reputation. At any rate, I don't answer the question during this introductory lesson.

I do explain what we'll be doing during the stream study. We'll divide into groups of three, each with a dipping net, a plastic spoon, a fauna identification key and checklist, and a white pan for collecting our catch. Everyone will get hip waders, with clear directions to not go above knee height. Each group will have a defined sample area marked off by orange pylons. After all, we're scientists, don't you know?

"I want you to stay within the area of your sample. Don't be concerned when another group catches something and gets excited. We'll see everyone's discoveries before we release our critters. Until then, stay in your area because you might be the only ones to catch a creature that other groups don't get."

I give my students a target number: ten.

"If, among all our collected samples, we catch at least ten different species, that's a very good sign of a healthy ecosystem."

※

The next morning arrives. We haul our equipment down to the river. I point out the trees lining the banks, and I can't resist asking, "Anyone see a trout in a tree?"

We set up the pylons. We review rules and procedures—for example, how to use the net to catch unseen creatures. And then they are totally engaged.

The excitement level is high. It's like we're on a lion hunt, only our quarry is much smaller—in most cases, smaller than a pinkie finger nail. There's no way we're going to catch a trout. Even if they're present, they are much too fast for our nets.

The classroom teacher and I move around from group to group, sharing in their successful finds, helping them with identification, and ensuring that everyone gets an equal opportunity to catch critters.

"Oh, and try to keep the water in your white tray as clean and clear as possible. If you get stones or mud in there, your creatures will try to hide by means of camouflage."

After thirty minutes of totally engaged catching, I ask the students to rinse their nets and place them together in a pile. We also line up our trays side by side, and we encircle them so everyone can see.

I let the students initiate a free-flowing conversation.

"Look at what we caught!"

"Wow, what's that?"

We identify. I tell stories.

"This stonefly nymph is a really positive indicator species all by itself," I say. "It only lives in very healthy ecosystems, and it's a favourite trout food. . . . Yes, even though we did not catch them, this is a great sign that trout are indeed here!"

"Hey, look! This nymph is doing push-ups! Since we've removed it from the flowing river, it needs to move the water past its gills so it can get enough oxygen."

Identification and stories continue. We count the number of different species we've caught, and it invariably surpasses our target. Our stream is healthy—we have biodiversity.

՟

We don't consider trees and trout until the evening follow-up session back in the classroom.

I ask, "If today had been really hot, where would you have gone during the stream study?"

"Under the shady trees," comes a reply. "It's cooler there."

I explain that creatures like mayfly nymphs and trout also need shade because only cooler water holds enough oxygen for them to breathe.

We then consider the tree roots. They hold the stream banks in place. There's no erosion of material into the stream. So, the water stays clear and clean and fast flowing. And the rocky stream bottom, where trout find stonefly nymph to eat and where they spawn, remains intact.

Oh, and one other thing: fish jump out of the water because they see a low-flying insect that's just taken off from the trees above.

We are noting all the connections. We are practising "ecosystem thinking." Trout need trees . . . and, actually, trees need trout. In British Columbia, dying coho salmon return to forested headwaters to spawn, and then their rotting carcasses provide much-needed nutrients for these trees.

And if there's ecosystem thinking, maybe there's also something called "ecosystem feeling." . . . For more on this concept, see my conclusion to the book.

A BIRD ON HAND

I am very frustrated. I can't for the life of me find the statistics I was once told about how long three-, five-, and seven-year-olds can stand still and how this time has markedly decreased for each age group over recent decades. Notwithstanding my foggy memory, I do have a powerful story that refutes the data.

One of my favourite wintertime activities is hand feeding chickadees when there's snow on the ground. These delightful creatures will form groups of twelve or so birds to forage for food. It's speculated that they learn from each other so when one soul boldly ventures onto the gloved and outstretched stick hand of a scarecrow (where I've placed black-oiled sunflower seed), the others work up their courage and also alight for a free "hand"-out.

❧

One day, I come snowshoeing by the scarecrow with a group of Grade 3 students who are fully mittened, scarfed, hatted, and wrapped in layers. They look like mini versions of the Michelin man. We are on a winter animal ecology hike, looking for wildlife and the different types of signs they leave behind.

The scarecrow is located near a clump of sumac trees where our feathered friends like to hang out. When we arrive at this figure, I ask the kids about the sunflower seed.

"Why is this here? Who is it for?"

I remove the seed from the scarecrow's glove, and I place it in my open hand. Then, I ask the kids to stand still and quiet while I move closer to the sumacs. I also stand still. I stretch out my arm. I make "phish, phish!" noises and then I wait.

Sure enough, our black-capped buddies arrive in the branches, quizzically calling to each other and perhaps to me. I wait. I continue to stand still. The little guys move closer and closer. And then, finally, one of them alights on my open palm and helps itself to a seed. I never tire of this intimate featherweight contact.

The kids are amazed, and they, of course, now wish to "try their hand." One student goes first, with others intently watching. The chickadee approaches. Just as it is about to land, the wide-eyed kid flinches . . . and the bird flies away. Undeterred, the kid resets, and, next time, she remains still and there's a successful landing. So cool!

Then I spread the kids along the edge of the sumac clump, each with seeds in hand. There's no trace of squirming impatience. They are willing to wait until they are rewarded. This blows those lost stats about the increasing restlessness of kids right out the window.

The nuthatch, tufted titmouse, and downy woodpecker are also known to hand feed, but they don't travel in groups, so your opportunities for hand feeding are much more hit and miss. Blue jays will not land on your hand, but one birder friend of mine has seen a jay dive bomb a chickadee so that its just-retrieved seed is dropped . . . and the blue jay then recovers it.

❧

At the Royal Botanical Gardens (RBG) in Burlington, Ontario, the feeding of chickadees (actually, all wildlife) has been banned. It became so "wildly" popular (the rise of Instagram really contributed to this) that people were bringing bags of cheap birdseed and, after their hand-feeding experience, dumping the remainder of the seed on the ground. This attracted opossums, skunks, squirrels, chipmunks, and raccoons. These animals are considered scavenger predators, as they will then go after turtle eggs as well as those of ground-nesting birds. Seemingly good intentions set off negative chain reactions. Once again, we see that "it's all connected." In the case of the endangered Blanding's Turtle, RBG officials are now obliged to collect their eggs and raise them in captivity for two years until they are old enough to fend for themselves.

Other wildlife urban areas have encountered similar problems, so this wonderful way of connecting with wildlife is now restricted to less public areas such as outdoor education centres and camps.

It's hard to beat a bird on the palm of your hand.

It's so up close and personal.

It's truly a moment of powerful connection.

DAWN WATCH

My digital clock reads 3:30 a.m. I rise noiselessly. My clothes and gear are all set out, ready to go. I don't want to disturb my fellow leadership staff in the cabin.

I meet Gail, my female resource councillor partner, by the lake. It's calm. The sky is completely clear. We're a "go."

We awaken our group of leaders-in-training (LITs). They are co-ed, fifteen to eighteen years of age, and from all over Ontario. They are sponsored by youth serving agencies—a camp, a school outers group, or an agricultural group like 4-H. The Ontario Ministry of Tourism and Recreation (later morphed into some other government branch) foots the bill for this transformative eighteen-day outdoor and environmental leadership training experience at what is now known as the Bark Lake Leadership Centre.

Our LITs already know the routine for the morning. Without disturbing others, they arrive at the dock with PFDs, whistles, flashlights, pillows, and paddles. They know that they are to remain silent until the sun rises.

Paddling partners lift and slide canoes from waterfront racks onto the water. We load up. We paddle off into the middle of our relatively small lake. We remain within sight of the entire group, and each craft has an assigned buddy canoe. The flashlights are only to be used in the event of emergency.

We are under a massive canopy of stars. Whoa! You don't see such spectacles back in the city. It's amazing. It's hard to comprehend. It's awesome.

It's a warm summer night. The air is still. There are sounds of distant frogs in an adjacent marsh. A loon issues a quivering call from a nearby lake. A whippoorwill is heard from the dark shoreline. There is a great peacefulness.

I am amazed at how soon the eastern horizon first lightens . . . but then it continues so slowly, so gradually, so timelessly. There is an extended period between first light and actual sunrise. Some LITs are sleepy and perhaps bored. They use their pillows, curl up, and fall back asleep. Others remain watchful and silent. It's their choice—all I can do is provide the opportunity.

Increasing bird song from the shores greets increasing light. Life is re-emerging.

Our silence is broken when the sun rises and an LIT greets the morning with his guitar and the little known but gorgeous John Denver song called "Summer."

We head to a nearby shore, facing the sunrise. We salute a new day with oranges and muffins.

Then, we head back to camp, still early. . . . Only a few folks are stirring. We make our way back to bed. It's time for a sleep-in.

❧

When we reconvene after lunch, it's time for a group meeting and reflections on our early morning experience. For those who chose to sleep, there's absolutely no judgement. . . . Even they are awed by what they experienced.

And for those who remained awake the entire time, it's hard to articulate impressions. Our group journal offers insights:

"I didn't think the sunrise could be so beautiful. It was like being in a different time and place entirely."

"We got up at 3:35 and staggered to Flagpole Point. Though we didn't get much sleep, we experienced something totally different. We saw the physical yawning and rolling out of bed of the Earth."

I can only hope that this experience becomes a lasting memory, a reminder that taking an occasional extended time-out in nature makes all the difference.

It seems that our government no longer gets it. "Fiscal constraints" led to the sale of this wonderful place in 1995. What a shame. Yet another short-sighted and ignorant step towards the extinction of outdoor experience.

MAPLE SYRUPING

For outdoor education centres in Ontario, Quebec, and New Brunswick, maple syruping is a time-honoured rite of spring. It starts when there's still snow on the frozen ground. It bridges the season of mud puddles, and it ends as the tree buds swell and the spring peeper frogs begin calling from forest ponds. It's a favourite time of year for both outdoor educators and visiting students.

The maple syrup operation at the Jack Smythe Field Centre, a day-visit centre run by the Peel District School Board, includes four distinct areas of activity.

ॐ

First (and last), there's a popular tractor-driven hayride. It's a great transition from the parking lot down a laneway to the sugar bush. What follows is not just a show-and-tell gig. It's very much hands-on.

ॐ

Along our history trail, students can learn about how our First Nations peoples discovered maple syrup. The process of boiling down sap (3 per cent sugar; 97 per cent water) to maple syrup (66 per cent sugar; 34 per cent water) and even further to maple sugar (what our First Nations actually did) was accomplished by transferring red-hot rocks via sturdy fork-shaped sticks from a fire into a hollowed-out log full of sap. With careful guidance from teachers, students get to move the rocks, hear the hissing noise of hot rock hitting sap, and see the resulting steam.

When European settlers arrived, they brought large iron pots with them, which meant that the sap could be boiled a lot faster. But all the related tasks meant that it remained a laborious process: collecting the sap in wooden buckets; gathering firewood; and boiling forty litres of sap into only one litre of maple syrup. All hands on deck. An all-out family effort.

ॐ

The next area to visit involves preparing the tree for sap collection. The first step is to be able to properly identify the rough greyish-brown bark of a sugar maple tree. Then, you use a brace and bit to drill a hole in the south-facing (sunny) side of the tree. This is frequently a two-person effort for our younger participants. One "braces" the implement against the tree while the other turns the handle around. Quite the determined effort . . . quite the teamwork!

We used to measure the diameter at chest height using a set of calipers. This determined the number of taps you can install on any given tree. The practice these days is that any tree over 20 cm. in diameter gets one tap.

Then you hammer in a metal or plastic spile (tap). Hang a metal bucket from the spile, then wait. If it's a mild day, the first drop comes within a minute. Reaching fingers capture subsequent drops and direct it into eager mouths.

"Hey, it tastes like water, with just a tiny bit of sugar in it!"

Finally, you install a lid to keep out the rain, moths, other insects . . . and persistent probing fingers.

As the tree buckets fill, you pour them into larger pails. It's great fun to watch primary-grade kids mightily haul these pails to the big tank by the sugar shack. Occasionally, it becomes a two-person effort, and the sap sloshes all over pant legs.

"Hey, you're sapping wet!" I exclaim.

Oh, and you also observe a modern and less labour-intensive method of transport where plastic tubing is hooked up to spiles running downhill to the holding tank by the sugar shack—kind of like a massive blood donor clinic.

And, oh, yes, there's wood cutting. This requires a sawhorse, a long pioneer crosscut saw, and four students. Two kids sit on top of the log to stabilize it on the sawhorse. The other two each grab a handle at the end of saw, and they take turns pulling it across the wood. Just pulling . . . no pushing. Once they get the hang of it, the sawing is very efficient. And, of course, everyone wants to give it a go.

❧

The grand finale is a visit to the sugar shack. You are greeted by a puppet named Maple-Roo, and in order to gain access to this building, you must sing the following to the tune of Polkaroo's song:

"The maple syrup door, the maple syrup door, Let's go through the maple syrup door! For songs and stories and so much more, Let's go through the maple syrup door."

The sugar shack contains a giant three-tray stainless-steel evaporator. The sap must make its way through channels in each tray from one end to the other. All the while, it is boiling away furiously and creating billowing clouds of steam, which escape through the vented roof. When the sap reaches the far end, you can tell it's become maple syrup using the following indicators:

- It reaches a temperature of 212 degrees Fahrenheit (seven degrees above the boiling point of water at sea level).
- The sugar hygrometer reads 66 per cent.
- As the syrup slowly drips off the end of a wood spoon/ladle, a "stinger" forms at the bottom of each drop.
- The colour has changed from clear and watery to a golden brown.
- It tastes like, well, absolutely delicious maple syrup!

Clean popsicle sticks are given out so that everyone can have a sample. No double dipping. The classroom teacher is also presented with a litre jar of our syrup to share with students on pancakes or ice cream back at school.

And, of course, we point out to our young visitors that all this is done "surreptitiously."

When I recently asked a sugar bush operator (C.K. Macdonald) who has been doing this for almost fifty years about the impact of climate change on maple syrup production, he noted two things. First, the season now starts earlier (March 1, in 2024 versus March 21, in the past). Second, the sap season is now broken up by more frequent and sudden changes in the weather.

Even though you want to maximize your maple syrup production, Macdonald notes that it's also important to preserve tree diversity for the overall health of a sugar bush. Monocultures are much more prone to disease, and they support limited wildlife.

A WALK IN THE DARK

"What's about to happen in a movie when it gets all dark and quiet?"

Grade 6 hands enthusiastically spring into the air.

"A fierce and angry bear is suddenly going to charge us!"

"The Slasher will emerge with a menacing cackle and a big-ass sword dripping with blood!"

"Freddie Kruger will terrify us into a frozen and helpless trance!"

"Wow!" I exclaim. "You guys have seen a lot of scary movies! Now, in a few minutes, I'm going to take you on a hike in the dark."

Even though we're at an outdoor school, chattering excitement and wildly imaginative what-ifs immediately follow. Once the hubbub begins to subside, I attempt to massage the tone.

"My goal is for you to not be afraid of the dark. My goal is for you to discover just how neat and peaceful it can be at night—that it's not a scary place after all. It's just Mother Nature at a different and fascinating time of our twenty-four-hour clock."

There are some head nods and murmurs. A walk in the dark has them both excited and a little on edge.

"Here's a few rules: I'm at the front. Your teacher is at the back. No flashlights"—this creates a surprised stir—"except for the teachers, who will only use them in the event of a safety concern. We will not scare each other. Instead, we'll try to relax and enjoy some great nighttime activities."

❧

Then, off we go. After a few minutes, I explain that our eyes have two kinds of sight receptors. We have cones, which detect colour, and we have rods, which see in black and white.

"Can you see the colour of my jacket? No, but isn't it amazing how much you can see in the dark with your rods? Wild animals are even better at this!"

We pause several times along the trail to discern the shapes of trees, a bend in the trail, and the occasional building.

We also pause to create a mini light show. In pairs, we take turns crunching down with open mouths on Wint-O-Green Life Savers. We observe impressive pyrotechnics in our partners' mouths. Very cool—and quite tasty, to boot. And there's even enough light created to activate the cones in our eyes and to, thus, detect a "northern lights" hue to the sparking effects.

At another spot, we place our cupped hands immediately behind our ears. Eyes widen as these improvised radar dishes suddenly detect the distant rushing waters of a nearby river. If you turn your head around like an owl, what other sounds can you detect? Perhaps the yipping of coyotes in the nearby hills.

Seemingly counter to the intentions of this hike, I reach into my backpack and pull out a Bluetooth speaker and an iPhone with an app of bird calls. I play the multiple and highly entertaining calls of a barred owl and I ask the kids to wait, in silence. The sequence repeats: more electronic calls, more wide-eared waiting.

And then it happens. There is a return call. This time, it's not from a Bluetooth speaker. The call repeats. The call comes closer. Then, we see the silhouette of an owl as it silently lands on a high branch in a nearby tree. The Bluetooth speaker continues the conversation.

Now, there's an entire family (four or five) of these curious creatures, high up in various branches, and replying with their full repertoire of calls. The kids are delighted and entranced. We are conversing with the wild.

The time then comes for a silent and solo walk. I send the teacher ahead some 200 metres. I ask my students to use their rods to motionlessly follow her for as long as possible, until she dissolves into the surrounding darkness. One at a time, I invite students to now follow the same well-defined trail to their teacher.

"I want you to be quiet. I want you to feel at peace as you slowly walk this clear part of the trail. Join your teacher at the other end and watch silently as your classmates arrive. If you're not sure about doing this, the first thing I want you to do is to wait and watch your classmates try this. If you are still not sure as we continue, you can choose to walk with a friend or with me at the very end."

The kids are totally into it. They remain quiet until the last student arrives at the far end. Then there is a lively outburst of chatter about how cool the experience was.

I smile in the darkness, hoping that these young souls have taken a positive step that brings them closer to their natural surroundings.

At the end of his poem *"A Child's Christmas in Wales,"* Dylan Thomas describes *"the close and holy darkness."* Maybe these students are now beginning to understand the sanctity that Thomas refers to.

MAGIC SPOTS

Magic: I use this word in my book title and again in this story. According to The Oxford Reference Dictionary, it has four distinct meanings, two of which are applicable here:

- *An inexplicable or remarkable (I would add "unexpected") influence producing surprising results*
- *An enchanting (charming or delightful) phenomenon*

For me, magic happens when there is a combination of fortuitous circumstance and a very open and willing subject. So it is with magic spots, a.k.a. solo spots.

A magic spot is safe, natural, secluded, and close at hand. With teacher guidance, it is ideally chosen by the student. Some type of portable waterproof seating pad is provided. No cells phones or other technology. No construction or other noisy distractions. Open to all, with age-appropriate guidelines.

Sitting in your magic spot requires quiet, patience, and an alert openness to one's natural surroundings. It is about peaceful mindfulness—not the usual mind chatter of what to do and what's coming next, but a readiness to take in the sights, sounds, and smells of one's natural surroundings.

With repetition, time, and patience, this solo spot can yield one or both aspects of magic. Consider the following observations from Grade 10 students who visited their locations over an entire school year:

"Out in my magic spot, I am quiet and relaxed. I don't worry about the things I need to do or anything else; I just sit. I think that is one of the main reasons why people care about nature, because it provides them an escape from their busy lives. When they find a place they belong or they feel safe, it becomes a refuge."

"For me, this was not an assignment to connect me to nature, but an assignment that led me to realize that these sacred places we hold in our hearts are everywhere and can be anywhere, and the only thing stopping us from making this entire planet our magic spot is our own minds."

"This spot has made me who I am. It belongs in me and I belong in it."

"My magic spot acts as a window into the ways that I feel and while I don't have anything figured out yet by any means that simple act of going and sitting somewhere in nature completes a small part of my being."

"Only with this magic spot did I realize that sometimes things lie dormant in your heart until you experience them, and then they feel exactly right. Every time I walk the path to my magic spot, I feel the familiar comfort of something deep within me responding."

"This spot has helped me prove this to myself: 'I Sense I Belong' was a sentiment I once thought was cliche and cheesy, but now I can say with complete honesty that I sense I belong here, not just in this spot, but in nature as a whole."

※

What more can I say?

the Magic Place

WHAT'S THE MATTER?

I am entirely garbed in white, except for a bright-red nose. I have long white ears on my head. I have white makeup on my face. I have a white lab coat on (with multiple layers underneath), and I have white pants. Oh, and I am wearing a pair of snowshoes over my white snow boots—all because I am Harry, the Snowshoe Hare . . . and it's January at the Upper Canada College Norval Outdoor School.

I am sitting by a fire, with a large metal pot nearby, a stirring spoon, and a large container of hot chocolate powder. There's snow all around, and the river behind me is frozen.

A class of heavily bundled senior kindergarten students descends the wooden stairs to where I am. They are here in response to an invitation that arrived in their classroom a few days ago. They are here to celebrate the birthday of the "Winter Wizard," and they are going on a hike to meet and help the wizard's friends who are immersed in feverish preparations for the big event. Oh, and there's one other thing: they have been studying "states of matter" back at school.

When they see me, I am seated on a stump and crouched over. I cover my eyes and begin to sob uncontrollably. On cue, the kids arrive and, all together, they say, "Harry, what's the matter?"

Between inconsolable sobs, I haltingly explain to them that my task is to make hot chocolate for the Winter Wizard's party. Only, the river is frozen solid, and so, "I can't get any water, and I just don't know what to do!" More sobbing follows.

Then one of the kids says, "Hey, Harry, why don't you put snow in your pot and melt it into water for the hot chocolate?"

I act dumbfounded. "You mean, we can take a solid—snow—and melt it into a liquid—water?"

The kids enthusiastically assure me that we can. They immediately take my pot and pack it with snow. We put it on the fire, and, sure enough, the snow begins to melt.

I am amazed and oh, so grateful, and the kids are oh, so pleased.

❧

Their guide then takes them farther on to meet Miss P.U., the black-and-white-striped skunk. She is also very upset. When they ask her, "What's the matter?" she explains that her birthday task is to inflate the party balloons. Only, she's trying to do so by putting rocks (a solid) in them. This is not working out at all well. The kids immediately explain that she needs to blow into the balloons . . . that she needs to put air into them. Miss P.U. is absolutely delighted with this revelation.

And then Harry rejoins the class and leads the group to yet another distraught party organizer, Nutty the Squirrel, complete with whiskers and upright busy tail. She is supposed to bring flavoured freezies to the birthday party. She's already got several flavours of juice but can't figure out how to convert these liquids into solids. The kids tell her to pour the juice into the little containers she has and then bury them in the snow. Technically speaking, this will not freeze the juice, but, well, you get the point.

As Harry leads the class from Miss P.U to Nutty and then from Nutty back to the outdoor school where the birthday party will be held, he calls out, "Party hearty! One, two, three, four!"

The kids pick up on the chant, and we walk together, in beat and in a single-line formation. Oh, what fun!

For lunch, there are plenty of colourful balloons, and, of course, the menu features hot chocolate and freezies. A white-bearded Winter Wizard shows up in full garb, and he's delighted to have all these young friends joining him for his birthday celebration. He gives evidence of his magic when the lights mysteriously go off and on; he also refers to recent weather events that he claims responsibility for.

※

Several months later, these kids return to Norval for another outdoor experience. As they go off on their hike, this time looking for signs of spring, they hear a voice way off in the distance:

"Party hearty! One, two, three, four!"

"Hey, it's Harry!" exclaims one kid, and they all listen intently.

Yes, the cycle continues.

※

Thanks to Trish Jamieson, a young (at the time) and very creative teacher at the Norval Outdoor School—she is responsible for this highly imaginative experiential program.

punching in at orienteering control...

ADVENTURE RUNNING

You are running through an open woodland on a fine spring day. You are looking for an orange-and-white marker that your map tells you is located on the western edge of a long, narrow marsh. You head along the top of a trillium-laden valley, keeping an eye on the stream that leads to the marsh. It's like a handrail. You start to see last year's cattails and bulrushes. You head down the hill and towards the far end of the marsh, and then—bingo! There it is! You feel very pleased with yourself. Planned action. Rewarding consequence. You use the punch dangling from the marker to prove that you found your target, then head off to the next control.

This is called cross-country orienteering, a.k.a. adventure running. As a young man, I became totally hooked on this pursuit. You take on the challenge of an entire course of ten or more controls. You are expected to find them in the assigned order, and you are timed from start to finish. At a top-level meet, there are eight different courses offered. They vary in distance and level of difficulty. The shorter beginner courses focus on humanmade features (e.g., buildings and trails) as well as obvious natural features like the western edge of that long, narrow marsh. The more advanced courses are all about reading the contours (lines that indicate a change in elevation) of a very detailed orienteering map. If you are serious about getting a good time, you will spend a lot of time off trail, relying on various natural features for your route.

In Europe (particularly Scandinavia), the top orienteers are considered elite athletes and are well known to the public. Events can be individual or team relay. The single largest event is the O-Ringen in Sweden: it lasts six days and annually attracts 15,000 competitors of all ages.

⁂

My personal love of orienteering also resulted in my taking a lead role in its development at the various outdoor education centres where I worked. I start with the Grade 4 Map and Globe Skills unit. You read a map in "Three-D": D for detail (the legend), D for distance (the scale), and D for direction (using a compass to line up the north arrow on your map with the north arrow on your compass; this is called "orienting" a map). With these younger students, I talk about "joggin' with your noggin'." I send them out in pairs, at first finding one control nearby and then, as their fledgling skills experience success, more controls farther away and more difficult to find. The teams are always quite proud reporting back to me. "We found them. . . . Give us more!"

It's a great lesson in cause and effect. They experience success at their own pace.

⁂

With older students, I spend a full day on orienteering. The morning includes the "Three-D" lesson, this time using a map that covers a larger area and includes a lot more detail in the legend. We do a group map walk, talking about and practising our techniques. We discuss handrails, attack points, and stoppers.

We talk about "cunning running," and this gets the competitive juices flowing.

The afternoon is set up like a real orienteering meet. Teams of two are sent out at timed intervals. There are staff with two-way radios at various control points along the way so that we can report each group's progress. The course is not complete until the team crosses the finish line and hands in their control card. The punch marks are checked. Their elapsed time is calculated by subtracting their finish time from their start time. The completed cards are posted on a long string, in order of elapsed time. And you don't know who the winner is until the last team has reported in. Student interest in how well they have done is clearly evident as they constantly check out the results.

※

I also tell my students about my friend Phyllis, a fellow orienteering enthusiast. Phyllis never ran. She walked and took in her surroundings, using the map as a way to discover new terrain and its occupants without getting lost . . . a life skill. Phyllis would come back when the prizes were being given out. And she would talk about what she had seen and enjoyed en route: the great horned owl that silently flew by her; the red fox that disappeared from the top of a ridge. If students chose to walk, I send them out with an earlier start so that they have more time to complete the course. It's their choice.

※

I take much pride in the high success rate of this program. It's yet another great way to expose kids to their natural surroundings. Action and consequence. Cause and effect. I remember this great orienteering sweatshirt—beneath a detailed map, it reads "Give me a map and I'm magic."

RACCOON CIRCLE

There is silence in the circle. Twenty-two Grade 1 students sit on the classroom carpet with their legs crossed. They stare intently at the open door of a small, blanketed cage in the middle of their circle.

A nose tentatively appears, then a black mask followed by ears. This immediately leads to numerous oohs and aahs . . . and this immediately leads to a complete disappearing act.

I don't say anything. The kids already know what to do. Quiet once again reigns, this time more permanent. And, one by one, three baby raccoons gradually emerge.

They do what raccoons always do. They use the soft, human-skin-like pads of their front feet to feel the carpet and anything else that comes within range of touch—a constant kneading motion—all the while looking about their surroundings, perhaps instinctively scanning for any nearby danger.

Their small circle of exploration expands. They encounter shoelaces, dinosaur socks and pink socks, and pant legs. There are many widened eyes and open mouths, and there is much muffled delight in the room. But the quiet still largely holds sway.

I take one of the baby raccoons by the scruff of the neck, just like Mom does. I bring her around to the students, allowing them, one at a time, to touch her fur and feel the bottom of her feet. I explain to my captivated audience that I am only temporarily looking after these young charges until they are old enough to be returned to a kindly veterinarian who looks after orphaned wildlife brought to her by concerned members of the public.

I sometimes get my charges when their eyes are still closed, and I feed them a baby mammal formula, first using an eye dropper, then a needleless syringe, then a baby bottle. As they grow older and more agile, I teach them to lap the formula with their tongues before I start adding scrambled egg and other mushy food to the dish.

The transition to a dry puppy kibble begins with Honeycomb cereal. This is my addition, and I imagine that the vet might not approve. They love to handle this sweet morsel with their tactile and dextrous paws before they chew away on one end, complete with surprisingly noisy mini munching. If my kits are at this stage when I visit a class, this causes great delight among my keen observers.

❧

When I take my young charges home, at first, they restrict themselves to the blanket-covered cage on the top stone step/platform at the back of my home. They seldom venture beyond the open door. But then, the entire platform becomes their stomping grounds, complete with rolling balls, plush toys, and the constantly available option to dart back into their cage.

Then, one little fellow ventures farther and stumbles awkwardly down the steps, with the others in close pursuit. Into my garden. Never out in the open. Always exploring. Incessant padding around.

Over time, their range grows to the entire backyard. A constantly checked fence keeps them from venturing beyond my property. The explorations continue endlessly. Mock attacks and chasing also increase. When I am outside with them, they follow me around like Mr. Mom, and they gladly cuddle in my lap.

They are getting their legs. They are learning to move and react like raccoons. When they are able to climb my back fence at about six or eight weeks of age, I know it's time for me to return them to the vet. She places them in a large outdoor enclosure with minimal human contact and a lot of other orphaned raccoons. They become more and more wild.

Then, at twelve to sixteen weeks of age, the raccoons are released into the wild at an undisclosed location. The vet initially brings food drops (more dry dog food) to them every few days until they no longer come back. Their insatiable curiosity and constant learning from each other inevitably lead to their independence.

I feel sad when I take my charges back to the vet. I shall miss these marvellous and mischievous critters. But there's always next year. There's always another batch of orphaned babies and thrilled-to-bits totally engaged kids. I feel so privileged to have both in my life. And, hopefully, my raccoon kin have not become obsessed with looking for Honeycomb trees.

LOOSE PARTS

In 1972, an architect by the name of Simon Nicholson developed what became known as the Theory of Loose Parts. He described loose parts as materials that can be moved around, designed, redesigned, and tinkered with. His thesis was that loose parts can create infinitely more opportunities for creative engagement than static materials and environments.

American child psychologist Louise Chawla enthusiastically adopted this concept, noting that nature is the ultimate and endless source of loose parts (e.g., soil, water, sticks, rocks or, with great care, small critters that don't bite) for children to actively engage with. As an outdoor educator, I have been a constant witness to this hands-on fascination.

※

A walk in the woods for primary students is never complete without loosely supervised exploration in small groups. A prime example is stopping to gently roll over a fallen log to discover what lies beneath: soft decaying wood, earthworms, centipedes, millepedes, potato bugs, and a moist, delicate salamander. The kids love to gently poke around and to feel living, squirming creatures in the palms of their hands. They love to share their discoveries and speculate on why this or that creature is in this particular spot. And at the end of our investigation, we are always careful to return our creatures and the log to its original position. I talk to them about the need for TLC: tender loving care.

※

A stream study is a big hit for all ages—living, moving creatures adapted for life in an aquatic world. Stories about how certain animals spend most of their lives underwater until this strange urge comes over them. They climb out of the water. They pop a hole in their exoskeleton by their neck, and then they climb out of their skin and fly away as an "adult" dragonfly, mayfly, or stonefly.

When I tell kids about this, I frequently end my explanation with "So, the next time your mom talks about how quickly you are growing up, tell her how, if you could be an insect, you would go into your closet, climb out of your skin, and fly away."

My timely advice always brings laughs and smiles.

※

Then there's our hands-on demonstration of a Grade 5 unit on simple machines and the forces they utilize. Take, for example, a hammer and a nail to be driven into a board. The action of hammering illustrates the power of a fulcrum—in this case, the force and motion coming from one's bending elbow. Well, you can't just have one student demonstrate this action. Everyone is compelled to drive the nail into the board. Unless you want to create a mutiny, there is simply no other option.

※

Perhaps the ultimate loose part is a stick, particularly for boys. They can be thrown. You can hike with them. You can build forts and shelters with them. With caution, kids can be safe with them. I smile every time I recall that the stick finally made it to the National Toy Hall of Fame (Rochester, NY) in 2008. Why did this obvious choice take so long?

❧

The most artistic example of utilizing loose parts is something we've done with intermediate and senior grades: the creation of temporary art using natural materials only, as per Andy Goldsworthy. After watching a video featuring this famous Scottish artist making gorgeous and painstaking creations, the students totally buy in. They are prepared to invest the time needed, and their final products are most impressive. Being made of natural materials, these creations are highly temporal. The only permanent record are photographs, of both the work in progress and in its finished form.

❧

Loose parts: they are everywhere, they're hands on, and they make for a wonderful assortment of engaged activities.

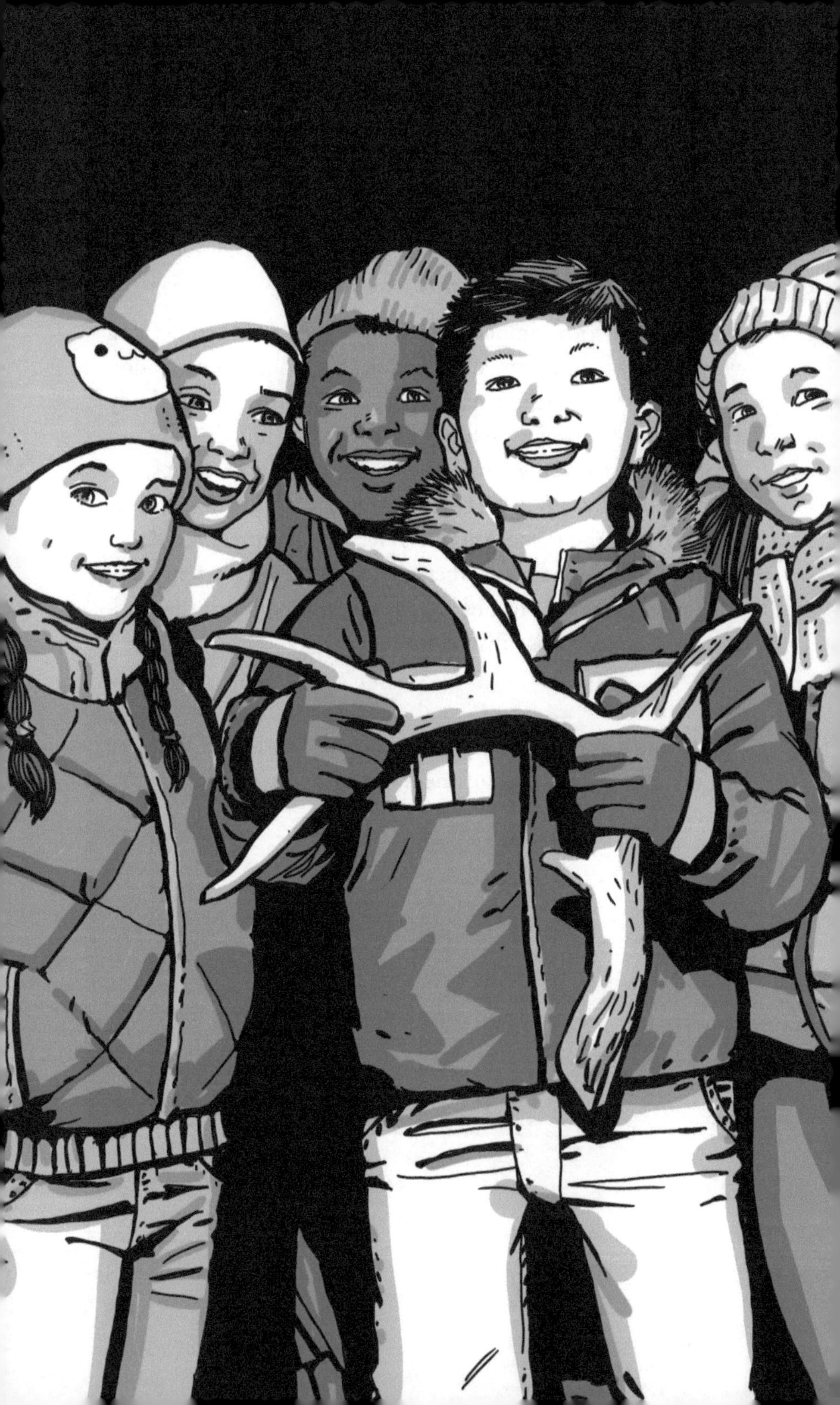

SERENDIPITY

The Oxford Dictionary defines serendipity as *"the faculty of making happy and unexpected discoveries by accident."* Unexpected—that's the joy of it, but one has to be ready to notice and indulge in such fortuitous circumstances.

My time as an outdoor educator has included many such moments, and I make sure to take advantage of these happenstance discoveries as much as possible. They are invariably moments of special connection. Here are a few examples.

❧

A Grade 7 class is walking to the remains of an old farmstead on our outdoor education property. We have shovels, trowels, whisks, string, and measuring tape. . . . We'll try to duplicate the conditions of a real archeological dig and see what we can find.

En route to the site, we come across a baby mouse, eyes still closed, lying all alone on the bare ground. This is not in the lesson plan, but it's a moment to be seized. I gently pick up the mouse and transfer it into the hands of a wide-eyed student I know I can trust. He holds it so gingerly, and the others crowd around. There is silence. There is stillness. This is a moment of unspoken connection.

Then, a student notices another mouse scurrying around, seemingly looking for something. We surmise it's the mother. I suggest to the boy holding the baby mouse that he slowly lower his precious cargo. Just before his hand reaches the ground, the mother mouse hops on, takes her baby by the scruff of the neck, and then she's gone. How cool is that!

A Grade 4 class is on a big property ramble, complete with a planned hot dog and marshmallow cookout. We hear a ruckus of crows off in the distance.

"There's a great horned owl nearby," I say.

The students look at me like I'm from Mars. I don't say anything more. We continue hiking, getting closer to the noisy crows. And then it happens. A great horned owl silently wings its way past us. We are all in awe.

Then, a mob of angry crows show up in hot pursuit.

I explain to my students that, during the day, great horned owls like to roost on high branches quite close to the tree trunk of a white pine tree. This effective camouflage helps them to avoid detection. But if a sharp-eyed crow happens to spot the owl, there's an all-call caw sent out, and, before you know it, there's this noisy gang of crows, bound and determined to chase away their mortal enemy. (Owls are known to prey on unsuspecting crows.)

Now, the kids look at me like I'm some genius naturalist. Not. Just lucky—and prepared to take advantage of this serendipitous moment.

A Grade 3 class is doing a "Who's been here?" animal ecology hike in the autumn. Given their energy level, we allow them to run ahead along an open trail until they see a handmade miniature red STOP sign. They know to apply their brakes and look for (but not go to) another handmade sign. This time, it's yellow and it has the words "Who's been here?" It's beside a nest, some fur, or some other evidence of animal life.

One of these spots has a furry ball right at the base of a large white pine tree. We examine the pellet closely and speculate the grey fuzz is indeed fur, and there are tiny bones also wrapped inside. We deduce that this neat package is the remains of a mouse. It has been eaten by a great horned owl. The owl's stomach then "burped" the waste material back up through its mouth, and, voilà: an owl pellet. On one occasion, I am interrupted in my explanation by another teacher:

"Uh, Mr. Linney, there's something high up in this white pine tree, and it's motionless, right up against the tree trunk."

Guess who?

❧

At another spot and another time on the Grade 3 "Who's been here?" hike, we find large scratch marks on the bark of a tree, around the face level of the students. We go through a host of possible explanations, gradually eliminating them for one reason or another, until we're left with the hypothesis that a deer was rubbing its antlers here. I explain that this is done in the fall to remove the velvet that's been growing on the antlers. Then the moment comes that I've been counting on: a pair of errant eyes spot an antler on the ground nearby. The kids are thrilled to bits with their find and with the connection that they have fortuitously discovered. Of course, I don't bother to tell them that I had discretely placed the antler out there before the hike. Who says serendipity can't be planned?

COAST TO COAST IN 28 DAYS

In the early 1980s, I spent my summers working for a Toronto-based travel agent who specialized in offering enrichment credit courses for high school students. My most memorable experience was taking twenty-four Grade 10 students from Charlottetown, PEI, to Victoria, BC. We flew to our starting point and flew back to Toronto at the end. Otherwise, our transportation was a combination of bus and train. Our accommodations were mainly university and independent school residences.

It was a jam-packed Canadian history/geography credit, so the kids didn't have any time for hijinks. It was both exhausting and exhilarating.

When I took on the role of course director, I interviewed students who had previously gone on this trip. The reviews were not favourable. Their arrival at various cities was marked by a senior citizens-type bus tour, complete with spouting tour guide. Not on our watch. I sat down with my two teaching colleagues, and we redesigned the course from the bottom up.

First things first: no early morning departures or late-night arrivals; these were teenagers, and they deserved/needed their sleep. Next up was to make the course as experiential and Canadian as possible. Here's a sampling of the things we did.

We had a choice of lobster or steak for our first meal in Charlottetown (unfortunately, most students chose the steak). We also saw Anne of Green Gables in that city's theatre. My favourite line from the musical occurs when there's a storm at sea and the ferries are not running.

"Oh, the mainland's shut off again," laments one islander.

In Quebec City, we had a member of the Parti Quebecois speak "en français." A bilingual student provided the translation.

Across the country, we ran our own bus tours, and the students had work sheets to fill out highlighting many of the settlement's features as well as its history.

In Montreal, an Anglophone from Alliance Quebec was our guest speaker. We also went to an Expos baseball game.

In Ottawa, we had one of the authors of the newly minted Canadian Charter of Rights and Freedoms as our speaker. And, of course, we visited the seat of our federal government.

In Winnipeg, it was a First Nations Chief.

In Calgary, it was a member of the Canada West Foundation. We also attended the Calgary Stampede.

In British Columbia, we went white-water rafting on the Thompson River as well as visiting Vancouver, Nanaimo, and Victoria.

Just before we boarded the plane back to Toronto, one student came up to me. At a loss for words, all he could say was a very heartfelt thank you. If I could read between the lines, I think that he, like his classmates, was quite amazed that we are all one country. Mackenzie King once said, "This country has too much geography," and I think we experienced this firsthand.

❦

As I recall this once-in-a-lifetime event more than twenty years later, I realize that I would now approach it quite differently. It would have much more of an environmental focus.

We would visit more national parks, and not just the historical ones like Acadia.

We would discuss Canada's plans to set aside targeted percentages of land and adjacent waters for natural preservation purposes.

We would examine the current and future impacts of climate change. We would interview wildfire crews, climate scientists, and noted Canadian authors such as Chris Turner and Seth Klein.

And once there were emissions-free air travel options available, we would also visit Canada's third coastline via Iqaluit. From coast to coast to coast . . .

STUDENTS ON ICE

*"We inspire and empower leadership
for a sustainable future."*

This is the mission statement for Students on Ice (SOI), a Canadian organization founded by Geoff Green. It provides young people with first-hand and life-changing experiences in the Arctic and Antarctic.

During the summer, international students from fourteen years of age to their early twenties gather in Ottawa for a three-day orientation program about what's to come. Then they take a chartered plane flight north—way north—to Resolute Bay, northwest of Baffin Island. In the past, some 120 young people and eighty staff board an ocean-going ship with a reinforced hull designed to travel through the ice. They're on this ship for the next twelve days, travelling through the Northwest Passage and across the Davis Strait to Uummannaq on the west coast of Greenland. The trip is completed when they fly back from Kangerlussuaq, Greenland, to Ottawa. On one occasion (2018) our starting point was Greenland, but conditions dictated that we had to turn back to our start because the ice was still locked in Resolute Bay. Ice conditions rule.

The program conducted during this journey is outstanding. Zodiacs with very experienced guides take students to several natural and historic landmarks, including bird breeding colonies, fledgling national parks (Qausuittuq, Quttinirpaaq, and Sirmilik), and the burial grounds for several members of the Franklin expedition. A marine biologist conducts an Arctic pond study; it includes the collection of water samples for microscopic examination back on the ship. Another scientist takes students to the foot of a large glacier and notes how much it has retreated since the last SOI visit. In Greenland, we visit an Inuit village with a world-class soccer pitch within sight of icebergs, and the students have a friendly game with the local youth. They also visit the Ilulissat Icefjord, a massive ice field and famous UNESCO World Heritage Site. Those staff who had been there before can't help but notice the ever-increasing amounts of meltwater amidst the ice. On some of the more remote field trips, guides with binoculars, rifles, and radios are posted in a wide perimeter around the students in the event that a wandering polar bear shows up.

There is also considerable learning on board the ship. A climate scientist shares the latest information on this existential crisis, particularly with reference to the Arctic. The then federal minister of the environment (Catherine MacKenna) discusses Canada's ambitious plans to protect 30 per cent of our coastal waters by 2030. Inuit elders demonstrate throat singing, tell stories, and drum dance. There are panel discussions and life stories. There are songwriting workshops with Canadian singer-songwriters like Ian Tamblyn. There are all kinds of artistic opportunities, including painting, print making, and journalling.

There is also the "bottle drop project," whereby sealed bottles are hurled by all participants (one at a time) from the stern of the ship into the Atlantic Ocean. If the bottle is subsequently found and opened, there is a message inside to please contact a Canadian federal government agency with the location of the find. This is used to track changing ocean currents.

Perhaps the greatest learning occurs in the interactions between students. Most are Canadian, but more than fifty other nationalities have also participated in these expeditions. A third of the students are Inuit, making for highly meaningful cultural exchanges with their southern neighbours. On one occasion, several students from remote Pacific island nations in danger of disappearing due to rising sea levels join the expedition and voice their unique concerns about climate change. Students share their observations and experiences in smaller groups (appropriately called pods) as well as during the all-participants recap session at the end of each day.

Another major feature of Students on Ice is the post-expedition follow-up. This is designed to transfer learning back home. There's a Facebook page for each expedition wherein photos and stories are shared. There's a steady stream of news from the Ottawa office, including opportunities to participate in subsequent international Arctic gatherings concerning the environment. This is a transformative program that keeps on giving. Its goal is to create globally minded citizens engaged in their communities.

IN THE SCHOOLYARD/ LOCAL PARK

It was more or less a last-minute make-work project. We had already hired additional outdoor education teachers for the Peel District School Board-run outdoor education day centres, but the new facilities were still under construction, and, thus, our new staff had nowhere to teach.

And so, for two full school years, our principal came up with the idea of "Outreach," where each of the field centre staff was assigned to a dozen schools. The idea was that we would offer hands-on outdoor education activities for primary grades locally, either in the schoolyard or in some patch of nature (e.g., a park) within walking distance of the school. This new mandate was not only intended to offer additional outdoor education programs but to teach children that nature is close by and to show classroom teachers that they could take more of a leadership role. I don't recall the field centre staff being overly enthused about moving from our established and familiar outdoor education property, but we did it—and we surprised ourselves.

❋

Our overarching and curriculum-based theme was animal habitat. We even created a song, complete with gestures, which the kids really enjoyed participating in. This was sung to the tune and cadence of "London Bridge Is Falling Down":

Food	[rub our tummies] and
Water	[make curvy waves with hands]
Shelter	[make roof over our heads]
Space	[stretch arms out wide]
Shelter	[repeat roof over heads]
Space	[repeat arms stretched out wide]
Food and water, shelter, space	[all four motions]
Make a habitat.	[hands come together]

Each time we repeated this song, we'd progressively go silent on a segment, only acting out the gesture. Ultimately, the entire song became an animated but silent series of gestures. The kids had great fun with this.

❋

Then we used puppets and stuffed animals to represent local creatures like the squirrel, rabbit, raccoon, wolf, and owl. I was always amazed at how totally engaged the students were with the puppet on my hand. The fact that this puppet was attached to my arm and my body, the fact that the puppet's voice was coming from my mouth—these features were totally ignored by the kids. They readily responded to the puppet's questions about how it finds food, water, shelter, and space at a particular time of year, and they even whispered secrets into the ears of my little furry (or feathered) friends.

And, of course, we played nature games that further reinforced our core concepts.

The kids would run around in a space marked off by orange pylons, pretending to be squirrels (short bursts of scurrying), rabbits (hopping and stopping), and raccoons (walking and constantly investigating). They would have to hide behind a tree or "freeze" if they heard the warning cry of a hawk (teacher), who'd then tag anyone who was still moving . . . or giggling.

In the fall, we'd bring acorns and beech nuts for the squirrels to hide for winter retrieval.

We also talked about animals who adapt to the coming cold weather by hibernating (e.g., raccoons and skunks) or by migrating (e.g., certain but not all birds).

In the winter, the teachers would hide wrapped candy for our hungry "creatures" to find. This was a definite motivation, but we didn't make it too easy for them to find their mini snack.

❧

Wolfgang, a.k.a. Wolfie, was our wolf puppet. He would introduce himself by saying, "Hi, I'm Wolfie! Do I eat peanuts, acorns, or candy?"

The kids would quickly correct him. Then, Wolfie would say, "Okay, so what do I eat? How do I find my meals?"

Often, sight was mentioned—looking for motion. Then we'd get around to smell, and we would test the kids' sense of smell.

"Can you smell the tree that has ketchup or onion rubbed on the bark?"

"What happens to your sense of smell if you wet your nose?" (Mammals keep their noses wet.)

※

Next up: "Hi, I'm Hooter, the snowy owl. What do I eat? When do I hunt? Unlike Wolfie, I can't smell very well.... That's why I don't mind eating skunks! So, what senses do I use to find my food?"

Yes, owls have great night vision. They also have fantastic hearing, with their flat faces acting like a radar dish to catch sounds.

We'd blindfold the kids and ask them to listen very carefully. "Can you point to where Hooter is hooting? Keep pointing and take off your blindfold. How close are you to pinpointing his location?"

※

After all these activities, we'd ask the kids to become squirrels again and see if they could find the peanuts they had hidden.... The success rate was often mixed, so we'd have some back-up reserves for those who were empty-handed.

Then, we'd talk about water—how it's found in the food that animals eat, in puddles, creeks, and ponds.

For shelter, we'd have rabbit pelts for our students to feel and examine and discuss how this fur is both waterproof and warm. If it was spring, we'd have bird nest "shells" and ask the kids to find nonliving materials to fill out the shell so that it was windproof and comfy. Then we'd compare their creation to some real bird nests.

For space, we'd have two kids stand within a hula hoop and try to play catch. If the ball went beyond the hula hoop, a teacher would have to retrieve it. When the kids started to get frustrated with this, we'd ask them which of the four habitat requirements they were missing and then play the game outside the hula hoop boundaries . . . much better!

So, we (the field centre outdoor educators) surprised ourselves. We learned that we were rather spoiled to always be working from an outdoor education centre, where all the props were readily available. And, like both the students and their classroom teachers, we learned that signs of nature can be found virtually everywhere. This was our most important lesson.

There was a goal beyond our provision of hands-on local outdoor experiences for students, and that was to motivate the classroom teacher to take their students outdoors within walking distance of their home school on a regular basis. We wanted teachers, with the help of accompanying parents, to feel comfortable taking kids outdoors to experientially reinforce curriculum concepts. As a supplement to this program, we also offered a series of workshops that provided a great variety of outdoor resources and activities.

FOUR CREDIT HIGH SCHOOL INTEGRATED OUTDOOR PROGRAMS

These are amazingly powerful and transformative outdoor programs. A co-ed group of students, mostly at the Grade 10, 11, or 12 level, stay together for an environmentally themed four-course package over an entire semester. This allows for the development of a powerfully caring community, both for each other and for the environment. One teacher is responsible for three credits. A second teacher handles the fourth.

Integrated programs are about making deep and powerful connections in nature, in curriculum and with each other. The subjects often include environmental science, civics, physical education, and interdisciplinary studies; other combinations exist. While the teachers are obliged to provide four distinct marks, every effort is made to integrate the courses so that students are enabled to apply different subject lenses to common themes. So, a Grade 10 science unit on optics (physics) will focus on nature photography, and the Grade 10 science unit on climate change will lead nicely into a civics unit on what to do about it. Grade 12 students in Guelph went so far as to organize a very well-attended public Town Hall on climate change, where they moderated a panel discussion involving the elected representatives from all three levels of government. They then directed questions from the public to the appropriate elected official. This was nothing short of outstanding civic engagement.

The teachers who run these programs are exceptional on so many fronts. They know their curricula and are highly motivated to integrate their subject areas wherever possible. They are passionate about the outdoors, and this seeps through their pores. Their outdoor skills are forged through personal experiences and high-standard certifications. Their people skills are outstanding: they know how to listen, when to step in, and when to step back. They are a very special breed of teacher.

These four-credit programs also create a very powerful learning community. Adolescents work, learn, and play together for full school days over the course of an entire semester. The fact that they are away from the daily distractions of a normal school day makes this community all the more focussed and intense. Words like connection, support, caring, friendship, belonging, honesty, truth, kindness, compassion, humility, wisdom, well-being, and even love frequently appear in student journal entries. Here's what one student had to say:

"My classmates became my family. We learned to support one another as we pushed each other to reach our full potential. I learned invaluable skills such as communication and leadership. I learned that I was stronger and more determined than I had ever known. I became open to new experiences and gained an entirely new outlook on life."

Another key part of the learning venue for these courses is the outdoor setting, ideally close to the school. Students are regularly outdoors over the entire semester. This is where much of their curriculum-based learning takes place. It is real. It experientially engages the head, heart, and hands—the whole person.

A series of overnight outdoor experiences (e.g., hiking, biking, and canoe tripping) are also offered, frequently increasing in distance away from the home school, duration, and challenge as the semester continues. This is invariably where transformational growth occurs. Students increasingly rely on each other for a wide variety of tasks required to make such trips successful. Among other things, they set up and take down campsites; they cook meals and clean up afterward.

Here's how one teacher describes these "peak" experiences:

"From an educational point of view, there is no better culminating environmental learning experience than a backcountry trip. Students get the opportunity to practise skills such as paddling techniques, building a campfire, and setting up a tent. They also prepare their own meals, filter water to drink, and monitor their waste; all accomplished by practising 'Leave No Trace' principles. And they have to do all this by working together. They learn that no one person is more important than the group."

❧

The connections the students make also extend to the natural environments in which they find themselves. While they are home-based, they experience weekly one-hour solos in the same location—time to observe, absorb, and reflect. When farther afield, their time outdoors extends dramatically. They learn to be warm and dry regardless of the weather. They take in gorgeous and changing natural landscapes. There are opportunities to watch sunrises, sunsets, and star-laden skies. There are also opportunities to observe wildlife (e.g., moose, porcupine) and to hear the calls of wolves and loons. Nature is up close and personal, the stuff of impactful memories and a lifelong caring environmental ethic.

❦

There is frequently a leadership component, where these students master the delivery of a single-day environmental program for younger grades. Knowing environmental themes well enough to teach them requires a whole new level of subject mastery. For the first time, many of these high school students see themselves as capable and influential leaders. The following observation from Katie Gad, an integrated programs veteran, bears witness to the teens' impact on younger students:

"I'll never forget coming across a Grade 10 student with his cool hat on backward and his jeans slouching down past his boxers; he was standing in a clearing holding a colourful maple leaf up to the light surrounded by a group of Grade 5 'wanna-be-cool-like-you' boys. They were looking up at that leaf with awe as they examined its veins and colours in the light . . . what power a moment like this has in a world where being 'cool' usually implies apathy and dissociation."

Moments of awe—these are the moments of deep connection that I am constantly on the lookout for, and what a joy to see a fifteen-year-old create this for a group of Grade 5s.

❦

That's what these integrated program packages are all about—authentic connections to program, people, and place, seeing things holistically, and caring for each other and for the planet.

PART THREE

OPINION PIECES ON THE VALUE OF OUTDOOR EDUCATION

INTRODUCTION
TO PART THREE

After a seven-year absence, I was deeply grateful for my fortuitous return to OEE in September 2000. When I was hired by Upper Canada College at their Norval Outdoor School, I felt like Lazarus arisen from the dead and I became driven to actively advocate for my profession. I became president of COEO, the Council of Outdoor Educators of Ontario. I led a rewrite of the COEO constitution that included a revised statement concerning the four unique, powerful, and lasting benefits of OEE. In 2002, I edited a theme issue of the quarterly Pathways journal put out by COEO. It was entitled "Voices from Outside Our Profession" and included compelling recollections of childhood outdoor education experiences from a variety of people now engaged in other careers. Between 2004 and 2006, I wrote three op eds about the value of OEE: one was published in the Toronto Star; the other two made it in the Globe and Mail. In 2007, I co-authored COEO's first research summary, entitled *Reconnecting Children Through Outdoor Education: A Research Summary*. It was filled with convincing evidence and compelling photographs of students actively engaged in OEE. It made specific recommendations, and it was targeted at key officials within the Ontario Ministry of Education. A group of us subsequently met with Kathleen Wynne, who was then Ontario's minister of education. We made a difference: additional funds were given to school boards specifically for OEE.

Flash forward. I retired in 2009, but continued to visit OEE groups and support the cause. In 2019, because OEE was once again regarded as a frill when times got tough, I co-authored another advocacy piece that was once again published in the Toronto Star. In 2022, I edited another theme issue of the Pathways journal, this time extolling the great value of school-sponsored canoe trips.

And now, this book. Yes, I remain driven. I remain possessed by the necessity of putting forth this most important message: if we wish to continue to live on this planet, we must reconnect—deeply—with nature, with the life support systems of this utterly unique and fragile entity.

Outdoor experiential education offers a powerful pathway to this; this section includes two of the opinion pieces I have written on behalf of our profession.

RECLAIMING THE OUTDOORS FOR OUR CHILDREN

Grant Linney

The Canadian wilderness has long been a part of our mental and cultural landscape. It was not that long ago that most of us grew up playing outside, in local woodlots and fields, in patches of untended nature that engaged our senses and curiosity for countless hours. In short, we used to be much more aware of our intimate connections to the outdoors and its natural systems.

Now our society has turned indoors and inward, as we spend more and more time staring at electronic screens and monitors. We are entranced by the lure of television, the internet, social media, video games, and cellphones. We are faced with the extinction of outdoor experience.

For a variety of reasons, we have also become increasingly fearful of outdoor landscapes that were once such a formative part of the Canadian psyche. We are told about diseases we can now contract, be they West Nile virus, avian flu, or Lyme disease.

We are increasingly confronted with what American author Richard Louv refers to as the criminalization of natural play. This is exemplified by the proliferation of "No Trespassing" signs as well as new regulations, procedures and liability waivers for all manner of outdoor activities.

But people are also starting to realize that there is a cost to such loss of contact with natural settings. In his book Last Child in the Woods, Richard Louv coins the startling term "nature-deficit disorder." He describes it as resulting in widespread human costs of alienation from nature, among them: diminished use of the senses, attention difficulties, and high rates of physical and emotional illness.

The first step in correcting this estrangement is to recognize it. But with equal urgency, we also need to realize and enact solutions. Letting go of our multiple and magnified fears will permit us to allow—and even encourage—our children to reclaim outdoor play as a natural part of growing up. Parents need to be with them, to spend time outdoors with their kids, modelling the curiosity and connection that they once hopefully had. However, even these steps are not good enough.

Just as we expect trained educators in our school systems to develop requisite language and numeric literacy, so, too, do we need to entrust them to develop the ecological literacy needed for a healthy and sustainable future. A large portion of this literacy must come about through the provision of safe and educational experiences in outdoor settings.

First, these experiences need to activate a child's natural curiosity and sense of wonder for her natural surroundings. Such experiences will provide the motivation to become advocates for the life support systems of this planet.

Second, they should provide compelling encounters with the intricacies and complexities of natural systems. Such encounters will greatly stimulate a student's critical thinking skills as well as their knowledge of the complex interrelationships of ecosystems.

Finally, these experiences will enable a child to see himself within the context of these life support systems, to examine and celebrate his natural surroundings from the multiple perspectives of a scientist and a geographer, an artist and a poet.

If, as polls suggest, Canadians consider the natural environment a priority concern for the healthy and sustainable future of our children, we must realize that they will not become its advocates and stewards through indoor lessons and electronic media alone.

We must bring them into the experiential midst of it. We must engage their senses through repeated and informed direct contact so that they can become the ecologically literate citizens that our planet so desperately needs.

※

A version of this article first appeared in the op-ed section of The Globe and Mail on September 5, 2006.[2] I have adapted it to fit the times.

---

2   Grant Linney, "Reclaiming the outdoors for our children, *The Globe and Mail*, September 5, 2006, https://www.theglobeandmail.com/opinion/reclaiming-the-outdoors-for-our-children/article731654/.

THE VALUE OF OUTDOOR EDUCATION

Grant Linney and Liz Kirk

While severe budget constraints are a current reality, we are saddened by recent cutbacks to outdoor education programs across Ontario. These include the termination of multi-credit high school integrated programs in Halton, Bluewater, Trillium Lakelands, and Simcoe school boards, the closure of four of ten outdoor education centres run by the Toronto District School Board, and the real potential for further reductions.

Outdoor experiential education (OEE) remains a powerful learning methodology for today's students. It embraces a wide spectrum of safe, teacher-led outdoor experiences.

These include regular neighbourhood walks, field trips to day and residential centres, and the aforementioned high school integrated programs, which can include cooperative education and specialist high skills majors (SHSMs).

Outdoor experiential education is not time away from school. Outdoor educators frequently refer to the butterfly model of learning. One wing is in-class preparation, getting ready for an upcoming outing. The body of the butterfly is the actual outdoor experience. The other wing is the follow-up that consolidates meaning and connections. Our butterfly cannot fly without all three parts.

In 2007 and again in 2018, the Council of Outdoor Educators of Ontario (COEO) commissioned comprehensive research summaries that highlight four substantial and lasting benefits of OEE.

Outdoor experiential education educates for curriculum. Students observe, measure, record, and assess within natural and urban surroundings. Its real-life, hands-on approach significantly broadens and deepens learning. This leads to more engagement and enthusiasm, increased proficiency in language skills as well as science, technology, engineering, and mathematics (STEM), and improved skills in critical thinking.

Outdoor experiential education educates for character. Its highly interactive nature spurs the significant development of both personal and interpersonal growth. Character traits such as creativity, self-motivation, assertiveness, and resilience are enhanced. Social skills are also developed; these include cooperation, effective communication, decision-making, and problem-solving.

Outdoor experiential education educates for physical and mental well-being. Research shows that time spent outdoors leads to a marked reduction in anxiety and an increased ability to perform positively in the face of adversity. This includes vulnerable youth. Time in natural settings also correlates with increased physical activity and fitness in children as well as the potential lifelong adoption of healthy and sustainable outdoor pursuits. Other improvements in well-being include reduction in the symptoms of attention deficit disorder as well as in high school dropout and crime rates.

Outdoor experiential education educates for environment. At a time when passive screen time dominates, outdoor education provides powerful first-hand encounters with our natural surroundings, a key first step towards developing a much-needed lifelong ethic for a healthy and sustainable future.

With all this evidence of substantial benefits (and there are more), we hope that Stephen Lecce, our provincial minister of education, recognizes OEE as an essential piece of what his government refers to as "value for money" and "education that works for you."

≈

Liz Kirk is the president of COEO (www.coeo.org) and an outdoor educator in the Niagara region. Grant Linney is a former president of COEO and is now retired from a career of outdoor education.

≈

A version of this article first appeared in the Toronto Star on July 15, 2019.[3]

---

3   Liz Kirk and Grant Linney, "The Value of Outdoor Education," *Toronto Star*, July 15, 2019, https://www.thestar.com/opinion/contributors/the-value-of-outdoor-education/article_182239f3-a468-5bce-b678-110f6c780008.html.

PART FOUR

OTHER VOICES IN SUPPORT OF OUTDOOR EDUCATION

Rachel Carson, scientist, environmentalist, author (from The Sense of Wonder, 1965)

It is not half so important to know as to feel. If facts are the seeds that later produce knowledge and wisdom, then the emotions and the impressions of the sense are the fertile soil in which the seeds must grow. . . . Once the emotions are aroused—a sense of the beautiful, the excitement of the new and the unknown, a feeling of sympathy, pity, admiration, or love—then we wish for knowledge about the object of our emotional response.

Tom Horton, American poet

We don't need a scientific breakthrough to tell us what to do. It's simply a matter of awe, of letting yourself stand in awe of it. And then the respect for how it's all connected and then working to curb our own wasteful ways.

David Suzuki, scientist, broadcaster, author, environmentalist

Leading scientists, including more than half of all Nobel Prize winners, tell us we are on a collision course with the life support systems of the earth. It is urgent that we understand we are still biological beings, embedded in and still dependent on the enormous services performed by nature for us. Nothing can be more important in an increasingly uncertain world beset by massive issues of climate change, toxic pollution of air, water and soil, deforestation, species extinction, marine devastation, overpopulation, overconsumption, and so on. These are the issues of our time and they have been created and made worse by our failure to recognize that we are still a part of nature. Outdoor education programs are invaluable for reconnecting children. . . . I think outdoor education is one of the most basic parts of education and ought to be a mandatory part of every curriculum in the country. It is not a frill or luxury; it is fundamental if we are to meet the real issues of our time.

Barbara McKean, Manager of Education Programs, Royal Botanical Gardens

Immersion in the outdoors, in experiences led by skillful outdoor educators, creates the opportunity for connection. Awareness and connection arouse curiosity, the desire to know more and the wish to understand. With this knowledge and understanding comes the desire to protect and to be a good environmental steward. Simple outdoor experiences for schoolchildren help lay the groundwork for an electorate that cares, that makes decisions based on principles of sustainability—decisions that don't mortgage our grandchildren's future to meet our own short-term needs.

Thomas Homer-Dixon, author, political science professor

Public funding of outdoor and environmental education shouldn't be seen as a frill that can be cut when budgets are tight. It must instead be a core educational commitment. The increasing disconnectedness of most of our young people from the natural world—young people growing up in urban landscapes of concrete, pavement, and fragments of managed nature—has practical, real-life consequences. Such children, when they mature into adults, don't have even a rudimentary understanding of humankind's intimate and infinitely elaborate relations with nature. And without such an understanding, they will not support—politically, economically, or socially—the protection of the natural environment on which humankind's survival critically depends.

CONCLUSION

When I was pursuing a mid-career master's of education degree, I was quite taken with a simple but profound truism: I teach who I am. The way I teach, the way I present myself to my students, is ultimately a reflection of what I care about. If I spend time in natural environments, this is apparent. If I am comfortable in natural environments, this comes through. If I deeply care about these environments, this belief is loud and clear.

In my story about trout needing trees, I wrote about ecosystem thinking—a.k.a. "it's all connected" thinking. I think there's another equally critical component here, and I call it "ecosystem feeling." It comes out of the following: letting go of our frenetic lifestyles and taking time to slow down, to absorb, and to feel an affinity for and connection/enchantment with our natural surroundings. This strikes me as a core part of a fully human person. Once again, I return to the words of theologian Parker Palmer: "To be is to be in relation." This is a basic tenet of science. This is a basic tenet of being human. This is a basic tenet of all life on Earth.

The stories that fill this book recount moments of powerful and lasting connection with nature. Research overwhelmingly shows that such encounters can lead to lifelong proenvironmental behaviours. If you directly connect, you care. You feel empathy and responsibility. You feel driven to act on behalf of our amazing natural world. You want to address the big issues like climate change. This will develop in you what Canadian author, adventurer, and friend James Raffan refers to as "knowledge of the heart." This is foundational. This is what drives you. This is what will save us.

ABOUT THE FAWN
ON THE FRONT COVER

After thirteen years of teaching there, June 1993 was my last month at the Jack Smythe Field Centre with the Peel District School Board. It was being closed due to budget shortfalls. In the midst of this sadness, we were given something positive and hopeful. A class of Grade 4s was just completing an animal ecology hike when a student at the end of the group came up to Jiiva, one of my teaching colleagues, and asked, "You know those stuffed animals you have in the indoor classroom? Do you ever put them outdoors?"

Jiiva paused, then said, "Well, no, we actually don't do that."

The student proceeded to show Jiiva a baby fawn curled up underneath some trees and immediately adjacent to the trail. Jiiva then signalled the rest of the class to come over silently. There were wide eyes and open mouths. Wonder. Reverence.

When the class left on their school bus, Jiiva instructed me to grab my camera and follow her. No further explanation was offered, but there was an imperative in her voice. "Oh, and leave Mr. Bill behind," she added. I readily obliged.

The fawn was still there. Once again, wide eyes and open mouths. Once again, wonder and reverence. And now, amidst the sorrow of immanent closure, a reassurance that the natural order of things would continue at this outdoor education centre.

As things turned out, the centre reopened within a year, this time with a much-reduced staff who were paid as uncertified teachers. I am very glad that the centre remains open to this day. And I am grateful to Jiiva for helping me to acquire an award-winning photograph that is still hanging on my family room wall—and now graces the front cover of this book. Can you see the mosquito?

ABOUT THE AUTHOR

climategrant@gmail.com   www.loveyourmother.ca

Grant Linney is an actively retired outdoor and environmental educator living in Dundas, Ontario, Canada. He holds a Master of Education in Curriculum Studies from the University of Toronto.

Grant has won several teaching and environmental awards at the municipal, provincial, and national levels. He is also a passionate photographer and video producer. He continues to give presentations and write newspaper opinion pieces about climate change.

Grant still loves to run team-building exercises with intermediate and senior grades as well as write and teach about outdoor experiential education. He continues to enjoy biking and canoeing.

Grant insists that he retains a lifetime membership in the International Save the Pun Foundation, even though the organization no longer exists.